Business Guides on the Go

"Business Guides on the Go" presents cutting-edge insights from practice on particular topics within the fields of business, management, and finance. Written by practitioners and experts in a concise and accessible form the series provides professionals with a general understanding and a first practical approach to latest developments in business strategy, leadership, operations, HR management, innovation and technology management, marketing or digitalization. Students of business administration or management will also benefit from these practical guides for their future occupation/careers.

These Guides suit the needs of today's fast reader.

Christian Rosser • Conradin Pfaff

The Sweet Spot of Legitimacy

A Manager's Guide

Christian Rosser
Swiss Institute for Translational and
Entrepreneurial Medicine
Bern, Switzerland

Conradin Pfaff
Bern, Switzerland

ISSN 2731-4758 ISSN 2731-4766 (electronic)
Business Guides on the Go
ISBN 978-3-031-15170-5 ISBN 978-3-031-15171-2 (eBook)
https://doi.org/10.1007/978-3-031-15171-2

© The Editor(s) (if applicable) and The Author(s), under exclusive licence to Springer Nature Switzerland AG 2022

This work is subject to copyright. All rights are solely and exclusively licensed by the Publisher, whether the whole or part of the material is concerned, specifically the rights of translation, reprinting, reuse of illustrations, recitation, broadcasting, reproduction on microfilms or in any other physical way, and transmission or information storage and retrieval, electronic adaptation, computer software, or by similar or dissimilar methodology now known or hereafter developed.

The use of general descriptive names, registered names, trademarks, service marks, etc. in this publication does not imply, even in the absence of a specific statement, that such names are exempt from the relevant protective laws and regulations and therefore free for general use.

The publisher, the authors, and the editors are safe to assume that the advice and information in this book are believed to be true and accurate at the date of publication. Neither the publisher nor the authors or the editors give a warranty, expressed or implied, with respect to the material contained herein or for any errors or omissions that may have been made. The publisher remains neutral with regard to jurisdictional claims in published maps and institutional affiliations.

This Springer imprint is published by the registered company Springer Nature Switzerland AG.
The registered company address is: Gewerbestrasse 11, 6330 Cham, Switzerland

Preface and Acknowledgments

This contribution to legitimacy management in hybrid organizations sprouted from previous research dealing with the legitimacy of hybrid organizations, which a team including Christian Rosser conducted at the *Swiss Institute for Translational and Entrepreneurial Medicine* (sitem-insel), the *KPM Center for Public Management* of the University of Bern, and the *Executive MBA of the University of Zurich* during roughly the last four years.

Hybrid organizations are fascinating organisms. For those working at the strategic level of hybrids, building and nurturing their organization is at once highly exciting and inspiring as well as challenging and exhausting. Metaphorically speaking, a hybrid organization must sometimes feel like a puppet with centrifugal forces pulling at its hands and feet in four different directions. In this context, organizational legitimacy—the subject of this book—is the sturdy thread that keeps the puppet from tearing.

Not only do we apply the term "legitimacy" in everyday life; it is also a complex concept with a long tradition in the social sciences and humanities. In strategy processes, legitimacy is more often than not used in its everyday sense to justify a certain goal or measure. Legitimacy is sometimes even used as a fighting term to sell something unpleasant with a more friendly face. A price increase or layoff, for example, can be legitimate. However, the fact that legitimacy can be considered and systematically evaluated as a more complex combination of different conditions of a hybrid's success is unlikely to play a role in the governance of hybrid organizations. Our concise book is thus a humble attempt to make legitimacy more relevant for the strategic management of hybrid organizations.

Even though legitimacy as a mirror of organizational success can hardly be handled with a one-page management summary, it does no good if it is perceived as mere showmanship from the academic ivory tower. Accordingly, we try to do justice to social scientific standards while at the same time taking into account the principle of managerial parsimony. We therefore believe that the book series *Business Guides on the Go* is the perfect outlet and hope that leaders of hybrid organizations may appreciate our findings as catalyst of their general reflections and discussions about the many challenges one may encounter during hybrid endeavors. At a more concrete level, our recommendations may be consulted, for instance, to formulate key performance indicators, create or revise business models, or for strategic communication.

The balancing act between scientific precision and practical digestibility is at the origin of our deliberate choice to refrain from a profound discussion of the extent to which our results complement or "correct" existing research and what future research projects might succeed our work. Rather, we want to focus our conclusions on practical applicability. In light of these considerations, we also do without meticulous theoretical and methodological considerations. We hope to pay sufficient but due respect to the scientific demands of our research field with what we present in terms of theory and method. What we do discuss from a methodological perspective is the personal involvement of one of the authors of this book in the establishment and further development of the sitem-insel. Considering that one author has since 2017 been a member of the sitem-insel's executive management and secretary of the Board of Directors, it seems inevitable that the interpretation of the data may take on a personal color at one point or another. On the positive side of the balance sheet, thanks to the personal involvement, there should be a profound understanding of the peculiarities of hybrids.

Finally, we would like to extend our wholehearted gratitude to those who have enabled and supported our research. The colleagues at the sitem-insel and especially Simon Rothen as well as Sabrina Ilgenstein and

Fritz Sager from the *KPM Center for Public Management* deserve special thanks. We would also like to express our appreciation to our interview partners from the sitem-insel and the Swiss Center for Design and Health (SCDH). We sincerely wish the representatives of the SCDH every success with their hybrid endeavor. Our additional gratitude goes to Ingmar Björkman, who has provided us with valuable inputs. We are also grateful to Angela Tschumi and Ramona Schindler for their help with the graphical representation of our guideline, as well as the team of the Executive MBA of the University of Zurich for their multifaceted support.

Last but not least, our affection and gratitude go to our loved ones who have supported us greatly.

About this Book

Emerging hybrid organizations face the challenge of gaining legitimacy. In order to provide executives with a strategic tool to address this challenge, we formulate a guideline that describes the sweet spot of legitimacy against the background of organizational science. We operationalize organizational legitimacy with the help of the three types of legitimacy: governance legitimacy, purpose-rational legitimacy, and value-rational legitimacy. Our qualitative-comparative study takes as its object of investigation two typical cases of hybridity—the *Swiss Institute for Translational and Entrepreneurial Medicine* and the *Swiss Center for Design and Health*. Our research suggests that the systematic combination of our three legitimacy types has the potential to optimize the level of legitimacy in emerging hybrids, thereby contributing to their success.

This book contributes to the *Business Guides on the Go* series by combining practical and theoretical insights into the complex topic of organizational legitimacy in an easily digestible form. It thereby provides decision makers, especially in the context of hybrid organizations, with leadership skills that work in terms of economic success in the marketplace as well as ethical accountability and integrity toward society. Thanks to our guideline, leaders of hybrids will be able to systematically manage the legitimacy of their organization in the future.

Contents

1 **Setting the Scene** 1
   1.1 Background 1
   1.2 The Relevance of Organizational Legitimacy 3
   1.3 Research Questions 3
   1.4 Relevance of the Research Question 5
   1.5 Structure of the Book 6
   References 8

2 **Legitimacy as Condition for a Hybrid's Success** 11
   2.1 What Hybrids Are and Why They Matter? 11
   2.2 What Organizational Legitimacy Is and Why It Matters? 13
   2.3 Finding the Sweet Spot of Organizational Legitimacy 16
        2.3.1 Governance Legitimacy 17
        2.3.2 Purpose-Rational Legitimacy 19
        2.3.3 Value-Rational Legitimacy 20
   2.4 The Affinity Between the Management of Organizational Legitimacy and Ethical Leadership 21
   References 24

Contents

3 Methodological Considerations — 29
  3.1 The Sitem-Insel and the SCDH as Typical Cases of Hybridity — 30
  3.2 Verification of Sources: How to "Measure" Legitimacy? — 32
  References — 36

4 The Journey of the Sitem-Insel and the SCDH — 39
  4.1 The Sitem-Insel: A Journey with Tailwinds and Headwinds — 40
  4.2 The SCDH: The Combination of Health and Design as USP — 47
  References — 52

5 Legitimacy Building in the Cases of the Sitem-Insel and the SCDH — 55
  5.1 Governance Legitimacy: Where Waterfall and Iteration Meet — 56
    5.1.1 Law Abidance and Political Accountability — 56
    5.1.2 Facility and Infrastructure — 58
    5.1.3 Leadership and Organizational Structure — 59
    5.1.4 Organizational Processes and Practices — 61
  5.2 Purpose-Rational Legitimacy: Defense Wins Games—Offense Wins Championships — 62
    5.2.1 Strategic Management — 63
    5.2.2 Financial Sustainability — 66
    5.2.3 Collaboration and Uptake — 69
  5.3 Value-Rational Legitimacy: Visualize Cohesion and Success — 70
    5.3.1 Social Mission — 70
    5.3.2 The Symbolic Appeal of Facilities — 71
    5.3.3 Dissemination and Validation — 73
    5.3.4 Team — 75
  5.4 The Legitimacy Guideline — 77
  References — 79

6	Conclusion	81
	References	85

Appendix A Empirical Strategy   87

Appendix B Interview Questionnaire   91

Appendix C Legitimacy Guideline   95

List of Figures

Fig. 2.1 Finding the sweet spot of organizational legitimacy. Source: Authors' own illustration — 17

Fig. 4.1 Relevance and Development of the Canton of Bern's Industry by Sector. Source: Adapted from Canton of Bern (2014a, 3). The location quotient on the x-axis measures the importance of the industry in the canton of Bern relative to Switzerland. The y-axis depicts the annual average growth 2009–2014. The food industry as well as the paper and printing industry are depicted as reference for comparison. The circles' diameter illustrates the share of gross value added (GVA) in the total economy, with the medtech and pharma circle representing approximately 1.4%. The shaded arrow and circle symbolize the political aim of the canton of Bern to 'grow' the pharma and medtech circle from the first quadrant to the second quadrant — 41

Fig. 4.2 Promoting and inhibiting milestones in the sitem-insel's development. Source: Own illustration. The figure provides a summary of the driving and inhibiting events in the development of the hybrid organization under consideration. The illustration is inspired by Lewin's (1973) "force-field analysis" — 45

Fig. 4.3 Promoting and inhibiting milestones in the SCDH's development. Source: Own illustration. The figure summarizes the driving and inhibiting events in the development of the hybrid organization under consideration. The figure is inspired by Lewin's (1973) "force-field analysis" 52

Fig. 5.1 Legitimacy Guideline. Source: Own illustration with the kind support of Angela Tschumi and Ramona Schindler. The two SCDH-related zero values are missing scores. It has been reported that a meaningful estimation of the relevance of the respective items is not yet possible 78

1

Setting the Scene

Achieving legitimacy is critical for the survival and growth of a venture.
Nagy et al. (2017, 50)

1.1 Background

With the aim of increasing the economy, effectiveness, and efficiency of the public sector,[1] policy makers in the Western world have since the 1990s promoted the provision of public goods and services in terms of market mechanisms, privatization, and entrepreneurial management (Kaboolian, 1998; Sager et al., 2012, 138, 2018, 22). Instead of the state's primacy, a concept of subsidiarity is applied today, according to which the design and implementation of public policies are to be delegated to "new modes of governance" (Heritier & Rhodes, 2010). Visionary slogans like "governance without government" (Peters & Pierre, 1998), "reinventing government" (Osborne & Gaebler, 1993), or "new public management" (Dunleavy & Hood, 1994; Pollitt & Bouckaert, 2004;

---

[1] As is customary in the literature, we use uppercase letters to refer to "Public Administration" as academic discipline, and lowercase letters to refer to the practice of "public administration."

Rosser, 2017) have dominated the discourse in both administrative practice and theory. At the same time, market and network-oriented forms of organization emerged as organizational principles, supplementing and partially replacing the bureaucratic tenets of hierarchy and authority (Weber, 1980 [1922]). Consequently, state administrations nowadays no longer exclusively provide public goods and services. Private companies or hybrid organizational forms such as public–private partnerships play an increasing role in the provisioning process (Hodge et al., 2018; Krog & Torfing, 2020; Rosser et al., 2021; Torchia et al., 2015; Warsen et al., 2018).

Hybrid organizations are fascinating objects of investigation (Denis et al., 2015; Doherty et al., 2014; Haigh et al., 2015). Battilana and Lee (2014, 397) define hybrid organizing "as the activities, structures, processes and meanings by which organizations make sense of and combine multiple organizational forms." It is the "duality of social and commercial logics" that characterize hybrid organizations (Bauwens et al., 2020, 197). Hybrids characteristically incorporate "multiple organizational identities," "multiple organizational forms," and "multiple action logics" or "rationales" from the public and the private sectors (Battilana et al., 2017, 133). Sometimes also called social enterprises (Vaccaro & Ramus, 2022), hybrids fulfill an important public purpose for today's society, for instance, in the fields of education, public health, research, and innovation policy (Gulbrandsen et al., 2015; Head & Alford, 2014). It is assumed that the structural diversity of hybrid organizations embodies one of their main advantages. For instance, the variety of know-how and skills among a hybrid's participants are supposed to allow for operational flexibility, mutual learning, and the sharing of resources. Hybrids should thus increase the efficiency in the provision of public services and goods by assigning the right professionals to the right tasks, using resources optimally, preventing waste, and reducing overall project costs.

However, at the crossroads between the public and private spheres, significantly more interest groups have a stake in hybrid ventures than in traditional corporate contexts. Stakeholders range, for instance, from employees through shareholders to customers and the general public (Siwale et al., 2021). Accordingly, we use "stakeholder" as an umbrella term and define it broadly as "persons or groups with legitimate interests in procedural and/or substantive aspects of [organizational] activity. Stakeholders are identified by their interests in the [organization], whether the [organization] has any corresponding functional interest in them" (Donaldson & Preston, 1995, 66). The fact that hybrid organizations have none less than civil society as legitimate stakeholder raises the question of how hybrid public service delivery affects traditional patterns of democratic accountability and institutional checks and balances (Koppell, 2006). In other words, questions about the legitimacy of hybrid organizations are key.

1.2 The Relevance of Organizational Legitimacy

Legitimacy is a fundamental requirement for organizational success (Díez-Martín et al., 2013; Dowling & Pfeffer, 1975; Zimmerman & Zeitz, 2002). Organizations with a high degree of legitimacy perform better and benefit from easier and sustainable access to resources. With legitimacy lacking, organizations may suffer sanctions from stakeholders, which in turn endangers the organization's very survival (Gulbrandsen, 2011, 221). Building organizational legitimacy is in itself a great organizational challenge that becomes even greater in hybrid contexts with a plethora of stakeholders having different identities, rationales, interests, and values (Rosser et al., 2021). Based on this understanding, we define legitimacy as a "generalized perception or assumption, that the actions of an entity are desirable, proper, or appropriate within some socially constructed system of norms, beliefs, and definitions" (Suchman, 1995).

1.3 Research Questions

While the body of theoretical knowledge about organizational legitimacy is vast (for an overview, see Díez-Martín et al., 2021; Deephouse et al., 2017; Du et al., 2022; Rendtorff, 2020; Suddaby et al., 2017), empirical studies dealing with the question of how emerging hybrid organizations may strategically influence their legitimacy are rare. In addition to empirical research about private organizations (Nagy et al., 2017; Scherer et al., 2013), we have preliminary insights into how emerging hybrids build legitimacy (Gulbrandsen, 2011; Huybrechts et al., 2020; Siwale et al., 2021). Our contribution builds upon this body of knowledge and the basic assumption of social contract theory, according to which organizations are ultimately accountable to the society for how they operate (Deegan, 2004). Furthermore, the present book represents a logical continuation of the work of the authors. Rosser et al. (2020) and Rosser et al. (2021) have thus far applied an organizational logic of different overlapping and mutually reinforcing forms of legitimacy to the single case of the *Swiss Institute for Translational and Entrepreneurial Medicine* (siteminsel) to examine what emerging hybrids undertake in their quest for legitimacy.

It is against this background that the book addresses both a descriptive-analytical and a consultative (or normative) research question:

- How do managerial attempts or the lack thereof affect the development of legitimacy in hybrid organizations during their emergence and early development?
- And how should the strategic leadership of a hybrid organization, such as the board of directors or the executive management, systematically and actively manage their organization's legitimacy?

In answering these questions, we aim to combine the theoretical body of literature with our preliminary empirical insights to provide a relatively simple ideal-typical framework—a guideline—of how to build legitimacy in hybrids. We underscore that we take an intraorganizational view of legitimacy management, because we want to address the practically relevant question of how to influence the legitimation process intentionally and actively and thus shape the path to a hybrid's success. We operationalize organizational legitimacy against the background of the three types of governance legitimacy, purpose-rational legitimacy, and value-rational legitimacy (Weber, 1980) and argue that the systematic combination of these legitimacy types has the potential to optimize the level of legitimacy in emerging hybrid organizations.

As regards the method, we apply two "typical cases" of hybrid organizations and subject them to a qualitative-comparative analysis in a "most-similar case scenario" (Seawright & Gerring, 2008, 297–298). More specifically, we compare the sitem-insel and the *Swiss Center for Design and Health* (SCDH),[2] two hybrids from the fields of research and innovation policy located in Bern, Switzerland. In terms of data, we on the one hand build on the authors' previous research about the sitem-insel mentioned above (Rosser et al., 2020, 2021). On the other hand, we have conducted three expert interviews with members of the SCDH's board of directors and executive management as well as one additional interview with a senior executive from the sitem-insel. We have complemented our body of data with neuralgic documents related to the SCDH.

1.4   Relevance of the Research Question

The relevance of addressing our research questions is at least twofold. From a practical perspective, it can support the strategy work of a hybrid leadership. We call for the intentional, systematic, and therefore more effective and efficient management of legitimacy as a critical factor for organizational success, especially in a hybrid's emerging phase. We claim that our legitimacy guideline can serve as a catalyst to prioritize the pursuit of success factors of hybrid ventures in terms of both content and time. The guideline may thus serve as a performance evaluation tool that supports managers in formulating strategic goals and subsequently controlling their fulfillment. We hope to thereby support managers to further develop their leadership skills—leadership skills that not only work in terms of economic success in the marketplace, but also in terms of ethical accountability and integrity toward society at large.

From a theoretical perspective, we aim to contribute to the embryonic state of research on the issue of legitimacy building in emerging hybrids. Our research may encourage a more comprehensive understanding of a relatively understudied topic, for instance, by complementing existing legitimacy typologies that are usually difficult to operationalize due to

---

[2] See www.sitem-insel.ch and www.scdh.ch (last access: 7.7.2022).

their high complexity. In contrast to these typologies, we argue that our three legitimacy types of governance, purpose-rational, and value-rational legitimacy are necessary and sufficient to operationalize organizational legitimacy. In a nutshell, we aim to formulate a guideline for the strategic leadership of hybrid organizations that meets social scientific standards while at the same time being parsimonious and simple enough to be practically applicable to the actual legitimacy management of hybrids.

1.5 Structure of the Book

This book is structured into six chapters (see Table 1.1). After the introduction, we in the second chapter derive the theoretical tenets underlying our guideline, which we gather from an overview of the literature on organizational legitimacy. As organizational legitimacy and organizational ethics are closely intertwined, we also provide a brief discussion of the latter. The literature overview leads into a fairly simple and therefore applicable tripartite legitimacy typology. We then discuss our method in the third chapter, before turning to our actual empirical contribution in the fourth and fifth chapters. Taking a dynamic perspective, we illustrate the emergence and development of the sitem-insel and the SCDH in the fourth chapter, before we apply our threefold legitimacy typology as analytical lens for the empirical comparison of our two cases in the fifth chapter. This empirical comparison leads into our practical guideline as actual core of our contribution. The guideline gives way to recommendations for concrete action that may support the successful strategy work in emerging hybrid organizations. In the concluding sixth chapter, we bring together the lessons learned, discuss their practical and theoretical implications, and discuss limitations of our study.

Table 1.1 Logic of argumentation

Chap.	Content (what)	Method (how)	Rationale (why)
1	Setting the scene	Descriptive	Introducing that the book is devoted to strategic legitimacy management in hybrid organizations
2	Theoretical underpinnings	Literature review (based on systematic reviews from the secondary literature)	Understanding the essential concepts of "hybrid organization," "organizational legitimacy" (with a brief discussion of "organizational ethics") Deriving a fairly simple threefold legitimacy typology
3	Methodological considerations	Descriptive	Qualifying the sitem-insel and the SCDH as typical cases of hybridity to allow for a valid comparison and (a limited grade of) generalization in the analysis Establishing transparency about the use of data and its interpretation
4	Dynamics of the two cases	Descriptive-analytical	Contextualizing the emergence and development of the two cases
5	Comparative analysis of the two cases Formulation of the guideline	Qualitative-comparative analysis	Gaining a sense of the mechanisms of legitimacy building in emerging hybrids through the lens of the threefold legitimacy typology in order to draw inferences for the guideline as a practical tool for the strategic legitimacy management
6	Conclusion	Descriptive analytical	Synthesizing the insights, discussing their practical and theoretical implications as well as the study's limitation

Source: Authors' own illustration

References

Battilana, J., & Lee, M. (2014). Advancing research on hybrid organizing. Insights from the study of social enterprises. *The Academy of Management Annals, 8*(1), 397–441.

Battilana, J., Besharov, M., & Mitzinneck, B. (2017). On hybrids and hybrid organizing: A review and roadmap for future research. *The SAGE Handbook of Organizational Institutionalism, 2*, 133–169.

Bauwens, T., Huybrechts, B., & Dufays, F. (2020). Understanding the diverse scaling strategies of social enterprises as hybrid organizations: The case of renewable energy cooperatives. *Organization & Environment, 33*(2), 195–219.

Deegan, C. (2004). *Financial accounting theory*. McGraw-Hill Australia Pty Ltd.

Deephouse, D. L., Bundy, J., Tost, L. P., & Suchman, M. C. (2017). Organizational legitimacy: Six key questions. *The SAGE Handbook of Organizational Institutionalism, 4*(2), 27–54.

Denis, J. L., Ferlie, E., & Van Gestel, N. (2015). Understanding hybridity in public organizations. *Public Administration, 93*(2), 273–289.

Díez-Martín, F., Prado-Roman, C., & Blanco-González, A. (2013). Beyond legitimacy: Legitimacy types and organizational success. *Management Decision., 51*(10), 1954–1969.

Díez-Martín, F., Blanco-González, A., & Díez-de-Castro, E. (2021). Measuring a scientifically multifaceted concept. The jungle of organizational legitimacy. *European Research on Management and Business Economics, 27*(1), 100131.

Doherty, B., Haugh, H., & Lyon, F. (2014). Social enterprises as hybrid organizations: A review and research agenda. *International Journal of Management Reviews, 16*(4), 417–436.

Donaldson, T., & Preston, L. E. (1995). The stakeholder theory of the corporation: Concepts, evidence, and implications. *Academy of Management Review, 20*(1), 65–91.

Dowling, J., & Pfeffer, J. (1975). Organizational legitimacy: Social values and organizational behavior. *Pacific Sociological Review, 18*(1), 122–136.

Du, X., Feng, F., & Lv, W. (2022). *Bibliometric overview of organizational legitimacy research*. SAGE Open. https://doi.org/10.1177/21582440221099524

Dunleavy, P., & Hood, C. (1994). From old public administration to new public management. *Public Money & Management, 14*(3), 9–16.

Gulbrandsen, M. (2011). Research institutes as hybrid organizations: Central challenges to their legitimacy. *Policy Sciences, 44*(3), 215–230.

Gulbrandsen, M., Thune, T., Borlaug, S. B., & Hanson, J. (2015). Emerging hybrid practices in public–private research centres. *Public Administration, 93*(2), 363–379.

Haigh, N., Walker, J., Bacq, S., & Kickul, J. (2015). Hybrid organizations: Origins, strategies, impacts, and implications. *California Management Review, 57*(3), 5–12.

Head, B. W., & Alford, J. (2014). Wicked problems. *Administration & Society, 47*(6), 711–739.

Heritier, A., & Rhodes, M. (Eds.). (2010). *New modes of governance in Europe: Governing in the shadow of hierarchy*. Palgrave Macmillan.

Hodge, G., Greve, C., & Biygautane, M. (2018). Do PPP's work? What and how have we been learning so far? *Public Management Review, 20*(8), 1105–1121.

Huybrechts, B., Rijpens, J., Soetens, A., & Haugh, H. (2020). Building legitimacy for hybrid organisations. In *Handbook on hybrid organisations*. Edward Elgar Publishing.

Kaboolian, L. (1998). The new public management: Challenging the boundaries of the management vs. administration debate. *Public Administration Review, 58*(3), 189–193.

Koppell, J. G. (2006). *The politics of quasi-government: Hybrid organizations and the dynamics of bureaucratic control*. Cambridge University Press.

Krog, A. H., & Torfing J. (2020). Legitimacy in co-creating governance networks. In *Handbook of business legitimacy* (pp. 401–417). Springer.

Nagy, B. G., Rutherford, M. W., Truong, Y., & Pollack, J. M. (2017). Development of the legitimacy threshold scale. *Journal of Small Business Strategy, 27*(3), 50–58.

Osborne, D., & Gaebler, T. (1993). *Reinventing government: How the entrepreneurial spirit is transforming the public sector*. Paperback.

Peters, B. G., & Pierre, J. (1998). Governance without government? Rethinking public administration. *Journal of Public Administration Research and Theory, 8*(2), 223–243.

Pollitt, C., & Bouckaert, G. (2004). *Public management reform: A comparative analysis - into the age of austerity*. Oxford University Press.

Rendtorff, J. D. (2020). *Handbook of business legitimacy: Responsibility, ethics and society*. Springer International Publishing.

Rosser, C. (2017). NPM und Public Value im Spannungsfeld mechanischer und organischer Staatsverständnisse. *Jahrbuch der Schweizerischen Verwaltungswissenschaften, 8*(1), 116–132.

Rosser, C., Sager, F., & Leib, S. L. (2020). Six recommendations to build legitimacy for translational research organizations. *Frontiers in Medicine, 7*.

Rosser, C. Ilgenstein, S. A., & Sager F. (2021). The iterative process of legitimacy-building in hybrid organizations. *Administration & Society*, 1–30 (early online). https://doi.org/10.1177/00953997211055102.

Sager, F., Rosser, C., Hurni, P. Y., & Mavrot, C. (2012). How traditional are the American, French and German traditions of public administration? A research agenda. *Public Administration, 90*(1), 129–143.

Sager, F., Rosser, C., Mavrot, C., & Hurni, P. Y. (2018). *A transatlantic history of public administration: Analyzing the USA*. Edward Elgar Publishing.

Scherer, A. G., Palazzo, G., & Seidl, D. (2013). Managing legitimacy in complex and heterogeneous environments: Sustainable development in a globalized world. *Journal of Management Studies, 50*(2), 259–284.

Seawright, J., & Gerring, J. (2008). Case selection techniques in case study research: A menu of qualitative and quantitative options. *Political Research Quarterly, 61*(2), 294–308.

Siwale, J., Kimmitt, J., & Amankwah-Amoah, J. (2021). The failure of hybrid organizations: A legitimation perspective. *Management and Organization Review*, 1–34.

Suchman, M. C. (1995). Managing legitimacy: Strategic and institutional approaches. *Academy of Management Review, 20*(3), 571–610.

Suddaby, R., Bitektine, A., & Haack, P. (2017). Legitimacy. *Academy of Management Annals, 11*(1), 451–478.

Torchia, M., Calabrò, A., & Morner, M. (2015). Public–private partnerships in the health care sector: A systematic review of the literature. *Public Management Review, 17*(2), 236–261.

Vaccaro, A., & Ramus, T. (2022). *Social innovation and social enterprises: Toward a holistic perspective*. Springer Nature.

Warsen, R., Nederhand, J., Klijn, E. H., Grotenbreg, S., & Koppenjan, J. (2018). What makes public-private partnerships work? Survey research into the outcomes and the quality of cooperation in PPPs. *Public Management Review*, 1–21.

Weber, M. (1980) [1922]. *Wirtschaft und Gesellschaft*. Grundriss der verstehenden Soziologie.

Zimmerman, M. A., & Zeitz, G. J. (2002). Beyond survival: Achieving new venture growth by building legitimacy. *Academy of Management Review, 27*(3), 414–431.

2

Legitimacy as Condition for a Hybrid's Success

The legitimacy and success of a hybrid organization are inextricably linked. Organizational legitimacy cannot emerge or will be compromised if there is a mismatch between the interests, values, and norms of the organization and its target groups. This implies that legitimacy needs to be considered and managed as a key objective in the strategy work of a hybrid. Accordingly, we in the following provide a more detailed definition and conceptual discussion of hybrid organizations, on the one hand, and organizational legitimacy on the other. Although hybrid organizations and organizational legitimacy are the two essential concepts of this book, this chapter also touches upon the issue of ethical leadership, which is an important part of the management of a hybrid's legitimacy.

2.1 What Hybrids Are and Why They Matter?

Hybrid organizations are typically the site of contestation, potential conflict, and negotiation over direction and strategy (Siwale et al., 2021, 453).

Hybrid organizations (sometimes also called social enterprises) are defined by their *combination* of (1) shared identities, (2) shared forms, and (3) shared rationales from the public and the private sectors (Battilana et al., 2017; Siwale et al., 2021, 452). First, hybrid organizations mix multiple organizational identities that define "who we are and what we do as an organization" and that "would not normally be expected to go together" (Battilana et al., 2017, 130). As Haigh et al. (2015) state in an interview with the *California Management Review*,[1] at the core of any hybrid organization lies a commitment to making positive social or environmental impacts." "To some degree," she adds, "hybrid organizations are an attempt to compensate for failures of the government." In contrast to private organizations, hybrids have a public purpose or social mission while at the same time pursuing commercial success in the marketplace. Hybrids thus face the challenge of bridging the tradeoff between their social mission or public purpose—e.g., the promotion of education, research, innovation, or public health—on the one hand, and financial sustainability on the other. To put it casually, it is quite simply not evident how to make money from a job traditionally performed by the public administration. Second, hybrid organizations combine multiple organizational forms such as networks, markets, and more traditional bureaucratic hierarchies. Hybrids are also characterized by shared ownership structures, which is important, especially when considering their various funding sources. Third, hybrids combine multiple rationales or beliefs and practices that shape behavior. In other words, multiple action logics may differ in the definition of what "constitutes appropriate behavior," and assumptions about "how to succeed" (Battilana et al., 2017, 136; cf. Rosser et al., 2021).

By implication, various identities, forms, and rationales within the same organization run the danger of goal incongruence. This is why hybrids "run the risk of confusing audiences and effectively catering to their needs, thus suffering a legitimacy discount" (Battilana et al., 2017, 142). Classical rational choice considerations point to problems of collective action (Downs, 1957; Olson, 2012 [1965]; Ostrom, 1990) that are to be expected in hybrid contexts. As hybrid organizations by implication incorporate disparate stakeholders, the probability of conflict within hybrids is greater than in purely public or private organizations with merely a public or private principal. Having to serve more than one

---

[1] https://cmr.berkeley.edu/2015/06/hybrid-organizations (last access: 7.7.22).

audience implies the great challenge of stakeholder management. For example, the maximization of benefits without the substantial contribution of individual stakeholders (i.e., freeriding) or duplications of efforts in the control and monitoring of different principles can lead to excessive costs (Sager et al., 2018, 22–23). What is more, unclear goals or lobbying by individual stakeholders may lead to inefficiencies and outcomes of the lowest common denominator (Rosser et al., 2021).

Recapitulating the state of research on hybrid organizations concisely, Siwale et al. (2021) hold that legitimacy is of utmost importance for hybrid organizations. They observe scholarly consensus that this is due to the heterogeneity of audiences and resource holders with potentially competing expectations that hybrid organizations must necessarily communicate with in order to gain their acceptance. Successful legitimation strategies thus underscore the importance of integrating multiple target groups, whose expectations are not necessarily complementary to the hybrid organization's performance.

Finally, none less than citizens are stakeholders in the hybrid provision of public services. Without established mechanisms of democratic voice and control, hybrid organizations are likely to have even more administrative leeway than their public cousins who function against the backdrop of institutionalized safeguards of political accountability. On the whole, it is because of their ambivalent reference systems of public state and private market that dealing with organizational legitimacy is crucial for emerging hybrids entrusted with the provision of public services (Rosser et al., 2021). Accordingly, we now turn to the theoretical underpinnings of organizational legitimacy. We thereby largely stand on the shoulders of two scholarly heavyweights: Max Weber and Mark Suchman (Langeraard, 2020, 423; Scalzo & Akrivou, 2020, 264).

2.2 What Organizational Legitimacy Is and Why It Matters?

Legitimacy has emerged as a pivotal but often confusing construct in management theory (Suddaby et al., 2017, 451).

Weber (1952, 1980) formulated one of the most influential conceptions of legitimacy. In fact, "most reviewers credit Weber with introducing legitimacy into sociological theory and thus into organization studies" (Deephouse et al., 2017, 30). Weber defines legitimacy as people's willingness to obey the orders of a ruler. Rule, in turn, is defined as the probability that commands will be obeyed.[2] A ruler enjoys legitimacy only if it conforms to formal laws and/or the social norms and values of its subjects. The institutionalization of rule is based on the establishment and cultivation of a belief in its legitimacy. Accordingly, legitimacy does not exist per se; it is a result of intersubjective valuing and reasoning (Rosser, 2018; Sager & Rosser, 2021).

When dealing with the legitimacy of organizations, Weber built on his ideal-typical view of traditional, charismatic, and legal rule. Weber's ideal-typical method means that scholars reduce the complexity of observed phenomena by arranging their components into analytical yardsticks that are meaningfully or rationally adequate. Scholars may then arrive at an interpretative understanding of complex phenomena such as rule by comparing an empirical observation with the ideal type (Rosser, 2018, 1013; Sager & Rosser, 2021, 5–6).

Ideal-typically speaking, Weber saw bureaucracy as the most effective form of legitimate rule from both an intra- and an extra-organizational perspective (Larsen, 2020, 132; Sager & Rosser, 2009, 1137). Even though he was primarily concerned with public organizations (Derlien, 1999, 58), he found little difference between them and modern private organizations, which he also saw as "unequalled models of strict bureaucratic organizations" (DiMaggio & Powell, 1983, 147). According to Weber, bureaucrats obey out of a conscious belief in the intrinsic value of complying with legal rules and procedures, whereas citizens weigh between ends, means, and side consequences before obeying in anticipation of success. The motives for obeying legal-rational rule are thus either value-rational, as in the case of the bureaucrats, or purpose-rational as in the case of citizens (Weber, 1980, 12; Sager & Rosser, 2021, 7).[3] Further

---

[2] Weberian rule (*Herrschaft*) has also been translated as domination or authority.

[3] The two concepts of purpose-rationality and value-rationality, which are essential for this contribution, are translated from the German Weberian terms *Zweckrationalität* and *Wertrationalität*, respectively.

distinguishing purpose-rational motives, Weber added that citizens would either obey in view of an organization's output (substantive legitimacy), or in view of how this output comes about (procedural legitimacy).

In line with the Weberian notion of legal-rational rule, organizational legitimacy may be conceived to mainly stem from formal or legal sources (Díez-Martin et al., 2021, 1). An organization then enjoys legitimacy if its actions are in line with applicable constitutional principles, legal rules, regulations, norms, and procedures. However, it would be inaccurate to attribute the legitimacy of any modern organization solely or even predominantly to its legal source. As Scott (1995, 45, *emphasis by the authors*) put it in his seminal book *Institutions and Organizations*, "legitimacy is […] a condition reflecting cultural alignment, normative support, *or* consonance with relevant rules or laws." For an organization to enjoy legitimacy, it takes for a social dependence of the ruler from the ruled and not merely legal chains of legitimation.

Almost as famous as Weber's conception of legitimacy is that of Suchman. As stated in the introduction, the latter defines legitimacy as "a generalized perception or assumption, that the actions of an entity are desirable, proper, or appropriate within some socially constructed system of norms, beliefs, and definitions" (Suchman, 1995, 574). In agreement with Weber, it follows from this definition that legitimacy is a social construct. While it is possessed objectively, it is created intersubjectively (Deephouse & Suchman, 2008, 54; Frostenson, 2020, 988; Zimmerman & Zeitz, 2002, 416). An organization's success depends on people's trust in the organization, as trust is the basis for the formation of stable relationships between the organization and its target audience (Rosser et al., 2021, 5; Scherer et al., 2013, 262).

Our reasons to use Suchman's definition of legitimacy are twofold. Not only is his relational and social constructivist concept widely used in the literature and generally accepted (Bitektine, 2011; Díez-Martín et al., 2021; Du et al., 2022; Rendtorff, 2020; Tost, 2011; for an alternative opinion, see Suddaby et al., 2017, 458). His definition is also contextual and culturally relativistic, thus applying to private, public, and hybrid organizations (Rosser et al., 2021, 3–4).

2.3 Finding the Sweet Spot of Organizational Legitimacy

Recent comprehensive literature reviews on organizational legitimacy show that organizational legitimacy is often analytically approached by means of sophisticated typologies (Deephouse et al., 2017; Díez-Martín et al., 2021; Scalzo & Akrivou, 2020; Suddaby et al., 2017). Suchman, for instance, distinguishes between "two temporal textures (episodic versus continual) and two substantive foci (organizational actions versus organizational essences), in order to arrive at a typology containing 12 distinct legitimacy types" (Deephouse & Suchman, 2008, 52). Whereas legitimacy typologies usually share Suchman's definition as starting point and more often than not refer to Weber's seminal work, they differ in terms of their research aim, question, and method, their sources of information, their micro-, meso-, or macro-level of analysis, their granularity, and so on. What the typologies have in common, however, is that they take a rather theoretical focus. Not only do they usually remain theoretical (Suddaby et al., 2017, 458), but the sophisticated typologies are arguably also too complex to serve as a guide for strategic legitimacy management in a practical environment (Frostenson, 2020, 986–987). In fact, the different types of legitimacy sometimes seem redundant, which adds to their limited practical applicability. This is a significant research gap when considering that organizational legitimacy is a vital determinant of organizational success (Díez-Martín et al., 2013).

We aim to formulate a typology that meets social scientific standards while at the same time being practically applicable. Following the principle of parsimony "as much as necessary, as little as possible," we argue that the three legitimacy types of governance, purpose-rational, and value-rational legitimacy are necessary and sufficient to operationalize organizational legitimacy (see Fig. 2.1). By doing so, we tie in with Díez-Martín et al. (2021, 3) stating that an organization's legitimacy rests upon the "justice" (governance legitimacy), "utility" (purpose-rational legitimacy), and "appropriateness" (value-rational legitimacy) of its actions. Evidently, the three types of legitimacy are overlapping and mutually

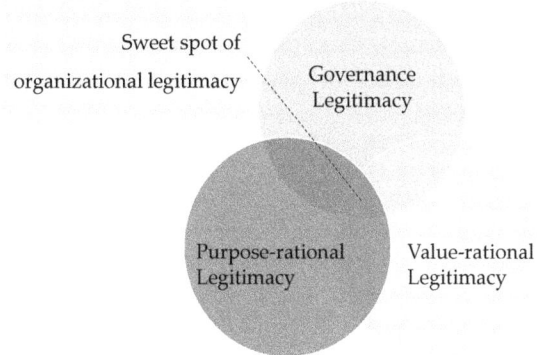

Fig. 2.1 Finding the sweet spot of organizational legitimacy. Source: Authors' own illustration

reinforcing. As Fig. 2.1 suggests, an organization's overall legitimacy increases, the more the three types of legitimacy coexist.

We refrain from discussing forms of legitimacy that have to do with irrationality. We assume bounded rationality instead (Simon, 1990), according to which people resort to so-called heuristics to make decisions due to cognitive limitations and imperfect information (Kahneman, 2003). In other words, people use problem-solving mechanisms or mental shortcuts that are usually based on simple rules. Bounded rationality is to be distinguished from irrationality, which refers to a deliberate violation of reason.

Especially when it comes to managing legitimacy from an intra-organizational perspective or "from the inside-out," we believe that our tripartite typology contributes to the strategy work in hybrid organizations. In what follows, we discuss what governance, purpose-rational, and value-rational legitimacy mean and how these forms of legitimacy occur.

2.3.1 Governance Legitimacy

When it comes to defining governance legitimacy, one has to be aware of different uses of the governance concept in Public and Business Administration. As mentioned in the introduction of this book, the concept of governance has become popular among Public Administration scholars to address new modes of political steering that go beyond traditional, state-centered forms of government (e.g., Benz, 2004; Kettl, 2015). From this perspective, governance spans the entire public sphere including "all processes of governing, whether undertaken by a government, market, or network, whether over […] formal or informal organization or territory and whether through the laws, norms, power or language" (Bevir, 2013, 1). On the other hand, the governance of private organizations—i.e. Corporate Governance (Hermalin & Weisbach, 2017; Larcker & Tayan, 2015)—is understood more straightforward as the set of rules, practices, and processes that are used formally to direct and manage a company. Hence, while Public Administration generally deals with governance from an extra-organizational perspective, the business perspective focuses on intra-organizational issues. In line with the latter view, governance legitimacy represents the most formal type of legitimacy, as it is concerned with organizational structures and processes for decision-making, accountability, control, and behavior within an organization.

Governance legitimacy refers to the formal organizational aspects of a hybrid (Blau & Scott, 1962). It concerns regulative, technical, and managerial formalities and occurs when stakeholders perceive organizational structures, procedures, practices, and leadership to be sound and professional (Díez-Martín et al., 2021, 5–6; Levy et al., 2009, 360; Rosser et al., 2021, 6; Suddaby et al., 2017, 454). This reminds us of Weber's procedural form of legal-rational rule (Meyer & Rowan, 1977, 342), according to which the legitimacy of an organization is assessed in view of how results are achieved. In a nutshell, governance legitimacy and "compliance" are close relatives. Both mean to make sure that a hybrid organization and its staff follow all applicable laws, regulations, standards, and ethical practices (Lengauer & Ruckstuhl, 2017).

It may seem evident that integer leadership and sound organizational structures, procedures, and practices play essential roles in building governance legitimacy. It may also seem obvious that the availability of necessary resources to staff critical organizational branches with proficient people who follow compliance guidelines is decisive for the administration of a hybrid. However, the systematic management of governance legitimacy in hybrids remains an understudied field. Accordingly, we will provide a detailed discussion of how the governance legitimacy of hybrid organizations may be influenced systematically and actively in the fifth chapter.

2.3.2 Purpose-Rational Legitimacy

Purpose-rational legitimacy is the most straightforward and pragmatic form of legitimacy, referring to a hybrid organization's instrumental value and utility of its output (Rosser et al., 2021, 5; Suchman, 1995, 580; Tost, 2011, 693). It occurs "when stakeholders clearly and precisely perceive benefits from the organization" (Díez-Martín et al., 2021, 5). Suddaby et al. (2017, 454) concur when they state that this kind of legitimacy "arises from an organization's capacity to achieve practical outcomes in its immediate environment." Being based on reason and self-interest, purpose-rational legitimacy parallels Weber's substantive version of legal-rational rule, according to which an organization's legitimacy is evaluated in view of its achievements. Simply put, the legitimacy of an organization increases when its stakeholders are better off after engaging with the organization or making use of its products and services than before.

The theoretical literature is largely void of specific discussions about the active management of purpose-rational legitimacy in hybrid organizations. However, several theoretical concepts exist that describe the emergence of purpose-rational legitimacy through the practical implementations the concepts entail. For instance, the emergence of purpose-rational legitimacy may have been portrayed as an unintentional byproduct of customer relationship management (Reinartz et al., 2004), customer advocacy (Meili, 2020), or the implementation of key performance indicators (Parmenter, 2020; Pozen & Kline, 2011). In contrast to these implicit portrayals, we will engage in a thorough and explicit discussion of how purpose-rational legitimacy may be built.

2.3.3 Value-Rational Legitimacy

Value-rational legitimacy comes into play because the legitimacy of a hybrid cannot be determined solely on the basis of factual-technical value chains. In addition to compliance with formal regulations and adherence to processes (i.e., governance legitimacy) as well as the factual outcome and benefit of an organization's deliveries (i.e., purpose-rational legitimacy), normative convictions as well as moral and social values held by stakeholders are crucial when it comes to building organizational legitimacy. Especially in organizations that depend on social cooperation in "complex and heterogeneous environments" (Scherer et al., 2013), such as hybrids, legitimacy depends on how much social trust these organizations enjoy (Torchia et al., 2015).

Value-rational legitimacy is the most subjective type of legitimacy, having to do with the comprehensibility and acceptance of the role an organization plays in its social environment (Deephouse & Suchman, 2008, 51). This type of legitimacy is based on the stipulation that action is handled with a certain normative conviction or value in mind, which in turn defines the action. According to Díez-Martín et al. (2021, 5) moral legitimacy is attained when organizations engage in actions that are stricto sensu not required, such as giving back to communities and larger parts of society. Simply put, moral legitimacy arises when organizations "do the right thing."

As hybrids must respond to the normative convictions and values of their stakeholders, value-rational legitimacy points toward the "importance of the relational dimension" of legitimating mechanisms (Tost, 2011, 703). Long-term loyalty and commitment between stakeholders and an organization are thus important sources of this type of legitimacy. What is essential is a sense of belonging, affective emotions, and relational identification. Value-rational legitimacy thus emerges in the context of social identification and manifests itself when "stakeholders assume that organizations represent the same values with which they feel identified with, and which they have in their minds and hearts" (Díez-Martín et al., 2021, 6).

On the whole, the presented understanding of value-rational legitimacy intends to reduce the complexity within the abundant typologies of organizational legitimacy that are tied to more subjective perceptions of organizations based on social norms, values, and emotional perceptions. By doing so, it builds on Dowling and Pfeffer's (1975) approach to judging legitimacy, which seeks congruence between actions of organizations and social system norms. This form of legitimacy can thus be contextualized as organizational behavior that is seen as "fair" (Aldrich & Fiol, 1994), "proper" (Massey, 2001), "appropriate" (Dacin et al., 2007), or "desirable" (Suchman, 1995).

Considering that value-rational legitimacy is the most subjective type of legitimacy, its systematic management is challenging. From a theoretical perspective, value-rational legitimacy aligns with concepts focusing on the establishment of an organizational culture as a set of shared values and assumptions that serve as "moral compass" guiding collective behavior and affect the way an organization interacts with stakeholders (McLaren, 1997; Ravasi & Schultz, 2006). However, concepts like corporate culture or corporate values, which are difficult to grasp analytically, have never been considered from the perspective of legitimacy management in emerging hybrid organizations. We attempt to contribute to filling this gap in the fifth chapter.

2.4 The Affinity Between the Management of Organizational Legitimacy and Ethical Leadership

Organizational legitimacy and organizational ethics are close relatives,[4] as they are both vital to organizational success. Research shows, for instance, that ethical leadership "fosters dedication, optimism, initiative, extra effort, altruism, better work attitudes and willingness of followers to help others with work-related problems" (Heres & Lasthuizen, 2012, 442).

---

[4] We use the term "organizational ethics" instead of "business ethics." For an overview of the current issues on business legitimacy and ethics, we refer to the *Handbook of Business Legitimacy* edited by Rendtorff (2020) as well as Bowie's (2013) *Business Ethics in the 21st Century*.

From a conceptual point of view, a hybrid organization resembles what Rendtorff (2020) calls an ethically and socially responsible cooperation, as both organizational models simultaneously aim at economic success and fulfilling a broader social mission. To put it in Rendtorff's (2020, 18) words, the "ethically and socially responsible cooperation […] is marked by an increasing willingness to search legitimacy beyond market criteria. This involves a focus on ethical norms and this means that the company is aware of a necessity of a definition of legitimacy norms in a socially oriented perspective. This company seeks to avoid doing things that are contradictory to prevailing social norms." The close affinity between organizational legitimacy and organizational ethics notwithstanding, legitimacy research and questions of ethical leadership have only rarely been integrated into the literature (Scalzo & Akrivou, 2020, 267). This may at least partly be due to the similarly high complexity of organizational legitimacy and organizational ethics.

Although an integration of organizational legitimacy and organizational ethics is beyond the scope of this chapter, it almost goes without saying that executives must address questions of ethical leadership when dealing with the legitimacy management of their organization (Brown & Treviño, 2006). We define ethical leadership as "the demonstration of normatively appropriate conduct through personal actions and interpersonal relationships, and the promotion of such conduct to followers through two-way communication, reinforcement, and decision-making" (Brown et al., 2005, 120).

Since the question of normatively appropriate conduct is a relative question, we would assume that ethical leadership depends on context (Frostenson, 2020; Goswami et al., 2021). Accordingly, we would expect ethical leadership to differ in private, public, and hybrid organizational contexts. Heres and Lasthuizen (2012) consider "publicness" and "privateness" as two extremes of a continuum, with hybridity in between. They determine an organization's position on this continuum by three different contextual factors, namely the form of funding, the extent to which public objectives are pursued, and the degree of political control. Arguably, these three contextual factors correspond to this book's three types of governance legitimacy, purpose-rational legitimacy, and value-rational legitimacy.

First, in terms of governance legitimacy, public funding and the resulting political-administrative supervision are essential. Beyond contractually binding performance agreements with the government, pressure from the media and interested citizens regarding the appropriate use of financial resources can narrow the discretionary scope of executives. For example, expectations regarding a transparent, fair, responsible, and accountable use of financial resources may compel a hybrid organization's management to heavily formalize "ethical compliance," incorporating ethical codes and regulations into the organization's governance in order to formally account to the public whenever necessary (Heres & Lasthuizen, 2012, 447).

Second, in terms of purpose-rational legitimacy, the requirement to achieve ambivalent goals is crucial. While private companies are focused on profit maximization, public organizations mainly serve the public interest. They provide public services and do generally not commercially trade them. With their intermediate position, hybrid organizations not only engage in favor of a public purpose, but also need to be commercially viable in pursuit of that very purpose. Given the tension between private market logic and public welfare, executives of hybrid organizations face the difficulty of keeping existing stakeholders engaged and attracting new stakeholders to the organization. In order to "sell" the organization and its services toward the outside, executives may feel the need to address ethical dimensions of decisions and actions more explicitly and frequently than their private sector peers (Heres & Lasthuizen, 2012, 446; McAlister & Ferrell, 2002). It is thus due to stakeholder inclusion that a hybrid's output incorporates a substantial ethical component.

Third, in terms of value-rational legitimacy, we assume that the self-selection of a hybrid organization's staff exerts an influence on ethical leadership. Studies on public service motivation (e.g., Ritz et al., 2020; Schott et al., 2019) suggest that public sector employees and, arguably, employees of hybrid organizations, feel a more pronounced desire to serve the public interest than private sector employees (Heres & Lasthuizen, 2012, 445–446). In comparison to giving back to larger parts of society, wages or other incentives working strictly according to economic utility maximization may play a subordinate role. In view of this intrinsic motivation of employees, we would expect that leaders of hybrids may consider it less important to frequently address ethical principles within their organization.

After having outlined the theoretical underpinnings of our book, we will now move on to our methodological considerations. In the following chapter, we aim to answer the question of why the sitem-insel and the SCDH represent typical hybrids and thus suitable objects of investigation for answering our research question. In addition, we address the question of how we have attempted to "measure" governance, purpose-rational, and value-rational legitimacy.

References

Aldrich, H. E., & Fiol, C. M. (1994). Fools rush in? The institutional context of industry creation. *Academy of Management Review, 19*(4), 645–670.

Battilana, J., Besharov, M., & Mitzinneck, B. (2017). On hybrids and hybrid organizing: A review and roadmap for future research. *The SAGE Handbook of Organizational Institutionalism, 2*, 133–169.

Benz, A. (2004). Governance—Modebegriff oder nützliches sozialwissenschaftliches Konzept?. In *Governance—Regieren in komplexen Regelsystemen* (pp. 11–28). VS Verlag für Sozialwissenschaften.

Bevir, M. (2013). *A Theory of Governance.* Berkeley: University of California Press. (escholarship.org)

Bitektine, A. (2011). Toward a theory of social judgments of organizations: The case of legitimacy, reputation, and status. *Academy of Management Review, 36*(1), 151–179.

Blau, P. M., & Scott, W. R. (1962). The concept of formal organization. *Classics of Organization Theory*, 206–210.

Brown, M. E., & Treviño, L. K. (2006). Ethical leadership: A review and future directions. *The Leadership Quarterly, 17*(6), 595–616.

Brown, M. E., Treviño, L. K., & Harrison, D. A. (2005). Ethical leadership: A social learning perspective for construct development and testing. *Organisational Behavior and Human Decision Processes, 97*(2), 117–134.

Dacin, M. T., Oliver, C., & Roy, J. P. (2007). The legitimacy of strategic alliances: An institutional perspective. *Strategic Management Journal, 28*(2), 169–187.

Deephouse, D. L., & Suchman, M. (2008). Legitimacy in organizational institutionalism. *The Sage Handbook of Organizational Institutionalism, 49*, 77.

Deephouse, D. L., Bundy, J., Tost, L. P., & Suchman, M. C. (2017). Organizational legitimacy: Six key questions. *The SAGE Handbook of Organizational Institutionalism, 4*(2), 27–54.

Derlien, H. U. (1999). On the selective interpretation of Max Weber's theory of bureaucracy. *Disembalming Max Weber.* Sophi.

Díez-Martín, F., Prado-Roman, C., & Blanco-González, A. (2013). Beyond legitimacy: Legitimacy types and organizational success. *Management Decision., 51*(10), 1954–1969.

Díez-Martín, F., Blanco-González, A., & Díez-de-Castro, E. (2021). Measuring a scientifically multifaceted concept. The jungle of organizational legitimacy. *European Research on Management and Business Economics, 27*(1), 100131.

DiMaggio, P. J., & Powell, W. W. (1983). The iron cage revisited: Institutional isomorphism and collective rationality in organizational fields. *American Sociological Review,* 147–160.

Dowling, J., & Pfeffer, J. (1975). Organizational legitimacy: Social values and organizational behavior. *Pacific Sociological Review, 18*(1), 122–136.

Downs, A. (1957). An economic theory of political action in a democracy. *Journal of Political Economy, 65*(2), 135–150.

Du, X., Feng, F., & Lv, W. (2022). *Bibliometric overview of organizational legitimacy research.* SAGE Open. https://doi.org/10.1177/21582440221099524

Frostenson M. (2020). Business legitimacy and the variety of normative contexts. In *Handbook of business legitimacy* (pp. 985–997). Springer.

Goswami, M., Agrawal, R. K., & Goswami, A. K. (2021). Ethical leadership in organizations: Evidence from the field. *International Journal of Ethics and Systems, 37*(1), 122–144.

Haigh, N., Walker, J., Bacq, S., & Kickul, J. (2015). Hybrid organizations: Origins, strategies, impacts, and implications. *California Management Review, 57*(3), 5–12.

Heres, L., & Lasthuizen, K. (2012). What's the difference? Ethical leadership in public, hybrid and private sector organizations. *Journal of Change Management, 12*(4), 441–466.

Hermalin, B., & Weisbach, M. (Eds.). (2017). *The handbook of the economics of corporate governance* (Vol. 1). Elsevier.

Kahneman, D. (2003). Maps of bounded rationality: Psychology for behavioral economics. *American Economic Review, 93*(5), 1449–1475.

Kettl, D. F. (2015). *The transformation of governance: Public administration for the twenty-first century*. JHU Press.
Langeraard, L. L. (2020). Public sector innovation, social entrepreneurship, and business legitimacy. In *Handbook of business legitimacy* (pp. 419–439). Springer.
Larcker, D., & Tayan, B. (2015). *Corporate governance matters: A closer look at organizational choices and their consequences*. Pearson education.
Larsen, Ø (2020). Max Weber's sociological concept of business legitimacy. In *Handbook of business legitimacy* (pp. 121–140). Springer.
Lengauer, D., & Ruckstuhl, L. (2017). *Compliance*. Schulthess Juristische Medien.
Levy, M., Sacks, A., & Tyler, T. (2009). Conceptualizing legitimacy, measuring legitimating beliefs. *American Behavioral Scientist, 53*(3), 354–375.
Massey, J. E. (2001). Managing organizational legitimacy: Communication strategies for organizations in crisis. *The Journal of Business Communication (1973), 38*(2), 153–182.
McAlister, D. T., & Ferrell, L. (2002). The role of strategic philanthropy in marketing strategy. *European Journal of Marketing*.
McLaren, R. I. (1997). Organizational culture in a multicultural organization. *International Review of Administrative Sciences, 63*(1), 57–66.
Meili, A. (2020). Bedeutung von Customer Advocacy in der Kundenbindung. *Digitale Schweiz*.
Meyer, J. W., & Rowan, B. (1977). Institutionalized organizations: Formal structure as myth and ceremony. *American Journal of Sociology, 83*(2), 340–363.
Olson, M. (2012) [1965]. The logic of collective action. *Contemporary Sociological Theory, 124*.
Ostrom, E. (1990). *Governing the commons: The evolution of institutions for collective action*. Cambridge University Press.
Parmenter, D. (2020). *Key performance indicators - developing, implementing, and using winning KPIs* (4th ed.). Wiley.
Pozen, R., & Kline, H. (2011). Defining success for translational research organizations. *Science Translational Medicine, 3*(94), 94cm20.
Ravasi, D., & Schultz, M. (2006). Responding to organizational identity threats: Exploring the role of organizational culture. *Academy of Management Journal, 49*(3), 433–458.
Reinartz, W., Krafft, M., & Hoyer, W. (2004). The customer relationship management process: Its measurement and impact on performance. *Journal of Marketing Research, 41*(3), 293–305.
Rendtorff, J. D. (2020). *Handbook of business legitimacy: Responsibility, ethics and society*. Springer International Publishing.

Ritz, A., Schott, C., Nitzl, C., & Alfes, K. (2020). Public service motivation and prosocial motivation: Two sides of the same coin? *Public Management Review, 22*(7), 974–998.

Rosser, C. (2018). Max Weber's bequest for European public administration. In The *Palgrave handbook of public administration and Management in Europe* (pp. 1011–1029). Palgrave Macmillan.

Rosser, C. Ilgenstein, S. A., & Sager F. (2021). The iterative process of legitimacy-building in hybrid organizations. *Administration & Society*, 1–30 (early online). https://doi.org/10.1177/00953997211055102.

Sager, F., & Rosser, C. (2009). Weber, Wilson, and Hegel: Theories of modern bureaucracy. *Public Administration Review, 69*(6), 1136–1147.

Sager, F., & Rosser, C. (2021). Weberian Bureaucracy. In *Oxford Research Encyclopedia of Politics*.

Sager, F., Rosser, C., Mavrot, C., & Hurni, P. Y. (2018). *A transatlantic history of public administration: Analyzing the USA*. Edward Elgar Publishing.

Scalzo, G., & Akrivou, K. (2020). Virtues, the common good, and business legitimacy. In *Handbook of business legitimacy* (pp. 263–275). Springer.

Scherer, A. G., Palazzo, G., & Seidl, D. (2013). Managing legitimacy in complex and heterogeneous environments: Sustainable development in a globalized world. *Journal of Management Studies, 50*(2), 259–284.

Schott, C., Neumann, O., Baertschi, M., & Ritz, A. (2019). Public service motivation, prosocial motivation, and altruism: Towards disentanglement and conceptual clarity. *International Journal of Public Administration, 42*(14), 1200–1211.

Scott, W. R. (1995). *Institutions and organizations*. Sage Publications.

Simon, H. A. (1990). Bounded rationality. In *Utility and probability* (pp. 15–18). Palgrave Macmillan.

Siwale, J., Kimmitt, J., & Amankwah-Amoah, J. (2021). The failure of hybrid organizations: A legitimation perspective. *Management and Organization Review*, 1–34.

Suchman, M. C. (1995). Managing legitimacy: Strategic and institutional approaches. *Academy of Management Review, 20*(3), 571–610.

Suddaby, R., Bitektine, A., & Haack, P. (2017). Legitimacy. *Academy of Management Annals, 11*(1), 451–478.

Torchia, M., Calabrò, A., & Morner, M. (2015). Public–private partnerships in the health care sector: A systematic review of the literature. *Public Management Review, 17*(2), 236–261.

Tost, L. P. (2011). An integrative model of legitimacy judgments. *Academy of Management Review, 36*(4), 686–710.

Weber, M. (1952). Die drei reinen Typen der legitimen Herrschaft. In J. Winckelmann (Ed.), *Legitimität und Legalität in Max Webers Herrschaftssoziologie* (pp. 106–120). J. C. B. Mohr (Paul Siebeck).

Weber, M. (1980) [1922]. *Wirtschaft und Gesellschaft.* Grundriss der verstehenden Soziologie.

Zimmerman, M. A., & Zeitz, G. J. (2002). Beyond survival: Achieving new venture growth by building legitimacy. *Academy of Management Review, 27*(3), 414–431.

3

Methodological Considerations

It should be noted at the outset that by method we do not mean methodology as the science of methods. In other words, we focus our discussion here not on the ontological and epistemological underpinnings of our qualitative research, but on the actual techniques we applied to obtain, analyze, and interpret our data. In the spirit of hermeneutic source analysis (Bowen & Bowen, 2008; Diekmann, 2002, 510–516; Rosser et al., 2021; Sager & Rosser, 2015), our method essentially involves the case selection, on the one hand, and the identification and verification of the sources we consulted to answer the research questions, on the other.

We will first discuss why the sitem-insel and the SCDH represent typical cases for a most-similar case comparison (Seawright & Gerring, 2008). We will illustrate that we have observed similar independent variables—i.e., characteristics of hybrid organizations—that help explain similar and/or dissimilar outcomes—i.e., degrees of governance, purpose-rational, and value-rational legitimacy. Subsequently, we discuss how we operationalized the three types of organizational legitimacy with regard to our concrete empirical cases (for an overview, see Appendix A). Our "source criticism" not only regards the credibility and reliability of the experts and written documents we consulted as primary data sources; it also addresses our personal involvement in the analyzed hybrids and the difficulties this involvement may pose for the interpretation of the collected data as "factual basis" for our research (Sager & Rosser, 2015, 206).

3.1 The Sitem-Insel and the SCDH as Typical Cases of Hybridity

The pharmaceutical, medical, and biotechnology industries are important pillars of a healthy Swiss economy and the preservation of Switzerland's healthcare system is of high political priority (De Pietro et al., 2015). The Swiss Confederation and the canton of Bern place heavy emphasis on promoting innovation in the medical and healthcare sectors. Both the sitem-insel and the SCDH receive subsidies under Article 15 of the Research and Innovation Promotion Act (RIPA), with which the Swiss Federal Council supports research institutions of national importance. This federal promotional measure is aimed at delegating tasks to service providers that are not performed by traditional institutions of the public sector. The federal financial support is subsidiary and complementary to that of the cantons and, potentially, other public and private parties (SSC, 2020, 4). In line with Swiss federalism and the concept of matching funds, both the sitem-insel and the SCDH receive another 50% subsidies from the canton of Bern. While subsidies amount to approximately CHF 61 million for 2017–2024 in the case of the sitem-insel, the SCDH applied for approximately CHF 44 million for 2022–2029 (Canton of Bern, 2021, 10; sitem-insel, 2021).[1]

In this context, both the sitem-insel and the SCDH qualify as typical hybrid organizations, as they combine (1) organizational identities, (2) organizational forms, and (3) organizational rationales from both the public and the private sectors. First, in terms of organizational identity, both organizations are characterized by the duality of a social and commercial identity. The sitem-insel as well as the SCDH find their social mission or public purpose in the field of innovation policy in the medical

---

[1] See also https://www.derbund.ch/22-millionen-fuer-swiss-center-for-design-and-health-in-bern-729569236169 (last access: 7.7.2022).

and healthcare sectors. The sitem-insel's social raison d'être is to promote innovation in the medical field, thereby contributing to strengthening the canton of Bern's medical location as well as Switzerland's international competitiveness (Frey, 2017; Ilgenstein, 2021, 10). In a similar vein, the SCDH strives to make the future healthcare system more efficient as well as economically, ecologically, and socially more sustainable in a design-based way (Canton of Bern, 2021). However, both organizations at the same time have to attain independence from public funding after a maximum of 8 years. The payment and use of the federal and cantonal subsidies are bound to performance agreements with the Swiss Confederation and the canton of Bern (Rosser et al., 2021).[2]

Secondly, in terms of organizational forms, both the sitem-insel and the SCDH are organized under private law as nonprofit corporations and present themselves as public–private partnerships. Their ownership structure consists of both public and private shareholders (Canton of Bern, 2015, 2021). This is also reflected in the hybrid composition of the two organization's boards of directors and advisory boards with members from private industry and public universities as well as political-administrative representatives. Moreover, both the sitem-insel and the SCDH are funding research staff from public universities in addition to the staff employed at their own corporation under private law. For instance, the executive management of the sitem-insel currently consists of the five "private" positions on the one hand, and one "public" university professorship, on the other (sitem-insel, 2022a).

Thirdly, both organizations must unite rationales that follow a rather distinct action pattern under the same roof. Arguably, the actions of executives following a managerial logic are quite different from those of professors following a rationale shaped by experiences and objectives of research and teaching. While the "private" managerial side predominantly acts upon the aim of generating financial revenue and orderly business procedures, more content-driven tasks related to research, teaching, and

---

[2] The most influential governmental bodies and political stakeholders of both the sitem-insel and the SCDH are the State Secretariat for Education, Research and Innovation (SERI) as well as the Swiss Science Council (SSC) at the federal level, and the Economic, Environmental and Energy Directorate of the Canton of Bern (WEU BE) as well as the Audit Office of the Canton of Bern at the cantonal level.

academic self-administration coin the actions of the organization's "public" side. What additionally unites the sitem-insel and the SCDH in this respect is their heterogeneous target groups from diverse scientific disciplines, industries, regulatory authorities, politics, and administration, as well as civil society at large (Rosser et al., 2021).

By identifying the sitem-insel and the SCDH as typical hybrids, we have prepared the grounds for comparing their development and legitimacy building mechanisms in greater detail. However, before turning to the actual empirical analysis, we have to set out what data we have based our analysis on.

3.2 Verification of Sources: How to "Measure" Legitimacy?

When attempting to turn our three abstract legitimacy types into measurable observations, we first addressed the *general* question of what data may allow for an assessment of a hybrid's governance, purpose-rational, and value-rational legitimacy. With *specific* regard to our two cases of hybridity, we subsequently asked ourselves how we might actually collect data in a parsimonious manner.

In general, governance legitimacy is easier to assess than the two other forms of legitimacy. This relative ease has to do with the accessibility of reliable information about a hybrid's facilities and infrastructure, its legal form, financial structure, and solvency as well as its formalized procedures to ensure law abidance and political accountability. However, governance legitimacy does not only refer to the general adherence to external requirements (laws, self-regulations, standards), but also to the existence of and compliance with internal regulations and directives in fields such as financial and tax matters, risk and quality management, ICT-related issues, or codes of ethical conduct (Díez-Martín et al., 2021, 5–6; Lengauer & Ruckstuhl, 2017, 7). Finally, the seniority of leaders and the qualifications and training of employees can be evaluated relatively easily with the help of social media platforms such as LinkedIn.

Secondly, if purpose-rational legitimacy is to be assessed, attention should be paid to stakeholders and their perception of the instrumental value an organization generates in their favor (cf. Deephouse et al., 2017). Therefore, direct situational exchanges between organization and stakeholders (Suchman, 1995, 580) or the fit between supply and demand need to be looked at more closely. If possible, perceptions should be "measured by asking stakeholders" (Díez-Martín et al., 2021, 8). If resources to conduct a stakeholder survey are lacking, the delivery of a hybrid's value proposition may be estimated with the help of expert interviews. Interview questions should then address various dimensions of performance such as funding, staffing, creation, external uptake, and collaboration (Pozen & Kline, 2011). Experts can thus provide valid information about a hybrid's "instrumental" output.

Third and finally, value-rational legitimacy is rather difficult to operationalize. With sufficient money and workforce, specific stakeholder surveys and polls can be used to estimate value-rational legitimacy, such as indexes measuring nonfinancial performance or public value (Meynhardt & Jasinenko, 2020; Spano, 2014). However, when resources are scarce, expert interviews and/or documentary analysis may once more be the method to resort to. When it comes to a hybrid's political stakeholders, for instance, parliament protocols are promising sources of information that are easily accessible. Moreover, it helps to ask the strategic leadership of hybrid organizations how they communicate with their stakeholders, and how they cultivate "soft-skills" related fields such as corporate culture and corporate social responsibility.

A stakeholder survey was not possible within the scope of our concise study. Not only is this due to the lack of time and financial resources; it also has to do with the limited access to the young SCDH's stakeholders. Another reason not to conduct a stakeholder survey is the personal involvement of the authors in the case of the sitem-insel. Not only would an extensive survey of stakeholders have exposed the authors strongly, thereby potentially affecting their daily job routine. Arguably, the interviewer's lack of impartiality would also have caused unusual problems of social desirability in the stakeholders' response behavior. Finally, a comprehensive survey could have influenced perceptions of the sitem-insel among stakeholders, perhaps causing the survey itself to have an impact on the level of value-rational legitimacy the sitem-insel enjoys.

In view of these limitations, we proceeded as follows: Based on our theoretical considerations and secondary literature on the one hand and the subsequent qualitative analysis of semi-structured expert interviews, numerous written primary sources, and informal conversations on the other hand, we formulated our legitimacy guideline. Consisting of items that operationalize governance legitimacy, purpose-rational legitimacy, and value-rational legitimacy, this guideline forms the actual core and main result of this contribution. The guideline ultimately permits us to answer our consultative (or normative) research question of how the strategic leadership of a hybrid organization should systematically and actively manage their organization's legitimacy.

More specifically, as regards the case of the sitem-insel, our research ties in with a previous study of the authors recently published in the peer-reviewed journal *Administration & Society* (Rosser et al., 2021, cf. Rosser et al., 2020) as well as research conducted as part of a doctoral project at the sitem-insel and the *KPM Center for Public Management* of the University of Bern (Ilgenstein, 2021). The data collected for these studies—i.e., 18 semi-structured expert interviews and slightly more than 3000 written documents stemming from an investigation period of 2008–2020—serve as rather a comprehensive basis for our analysis of the sitem-insel case. The interviews, which lasted about one hour each, were led by both internal stakeholders at the senior-executive level of the sitem-insel and external stakeholders including the federal and the cantonal government. For the sake of readability, we in the empirical Chaps. 4 and 5 refrain from referencing the primary sources and interviews collected in the course of the abovementioned research about the sitem-insel. We merely refer to sitem-insel-related primary sources when they were not used by Rosser et al. (2021).

Although Rosser et al. (2021) addressed questions regarding the strategy work and developmental milestones of the sitem-insel during their expert interviews, it should be underscored that the questions neither implicitly nor explicitly had a direct link to the three types of governance, purpose-rational, and value-rational legitimacy. These types were first formulated for this book instead, which is at least partly due to a certain reservation about the practical applicability of the preceding work. What follows thus represents our reinterpretation of the beforementioned work through our new tripartite analytical lens.

As a member of the sitem-insel's executive management and secretary of the Board of Directors, one of the authors of this contribution has since early 2017 been a first-hand witness to what is being analyzed and interpreted here. In view of this personal involvement in one of the empirical cases, it almost goes without saying that the authors are themselves a primary source of data. Attention must therefore be drawn to the so-called "involvement paradox" (Langley & Klag, 2019, 515). On the one hand, field proximity is a fundamental principle and quality feature of qualitative research, as the substantial expertise of involved authors increases their understanding of within-case complexity and thus the validity of the case analysis. On the other hand, skepticism prevails about the lack of professional distance of a social scientist and the resulting corruption of research results. However, the fact that the 18 interviews about the sitem-insel were not led by any of the authors of this book increases the validity of our research. Other than that, we trust that it is best to take due account of our personal involvement by distinguishing our empirical analysis and our personal assessment in the empirical chapters with the help of linguistic formulations such as "we argue" and "we believe."

In the case of the SCDH, we proceeded in a similar manner as in the case of the sitem-insel to ensure the comparability of our data. We once more consulted publicly available documents such as newspaper articles, parliamentary minutes, and Internet publications. Moreover, we conducted two expert interviews of a duration of approximately one hour each. The two interviews with one member of the Board of Directors and one member of the executive management, respectively, will be referenced in the following as interview 1 and interview 2. As in the case of the sitem-insel, the three legitimacy types were not addressed explicitly during our interviews (see Appendix B). Finally, we were able to supplement our interviews with the help of several informal exchanges.

The comparative validity of our analysis is enhanced by the fact that one of our interviewees sits on the Board of Directors of both hybrid organizations studied here. However, this aspect at the same time points to Galton's problem as potential limitation of our study. Against the danger of oversimplification, Galton's problem has to do with two units of investigation actually influencing each other instead of being independent (Naroll, 1965). As will become clear in the next chapter, the SCDH's development is anything else than independent from that of the sitem-insel. Not only our interviewees, but also the parliament protocols clearly suggest that the SCDH witnessed both advantages and disadvantages in its emergence and development because of internal and external stakeholders' frequent comparisons between the two centers.

We were able to finalize our qualitative-comparative analysis by the end of October 2021 and two derive our guidelines from our analysis until mid-November 2021. This in turn allowed us to subject the guideline to a preliminary "field test" in late November. In the course of two further interviews of approximately one hour each, we asked one member of the strategic leadership of each the SCDH (i.e., Interview 3) and the sitem-insel (i.e., Interview 4) to rate the relevance of our guideline's items for the success of their respective organization. Without being asked, our interviewees noticed that the individual elements they were questioned about were all important for the success of their organization, which can be seen as a first careful confirmation of our guideline's construct validity. Finally, when preparing the manuscript for publication in 2022, we consulted the sitem-insel's official annual report 2021 and the political reporting dossier 2021 (sitem-insel, 2022a, 2022b) as well as the latest information available on the SCDH's website.[3] It should be noted that we mainly consulted these sources to update figures. It should also be mentioned that our interviews were led in German and that all written primary sources are either in German or in French. Accordingly, all translations and potential mistranslations made here are our own.

References

Bowen, C. C., & Bowen, W. M. (2008). Content analysis. In K. Yang & G. J. Miller (Eds.), *Handbook of research methods in public administration* (pp. 689–704). CRC Press.

---

[3] See www.scdh.ch (last access: 7.7.2022).

Canton of Bern. (2015, October 14). *Vortrag der Volkswirtschaftsdirektion*. Dok.-Nr.: 81478.

Canton of Bern. (2021, May 12). *Vortrag der Wirtschafts-,* Energie- und Umweltdirektion. Geschäftsnummer 2021.WEU.256.

De Pietro, C., Camenzind, P., Sturny, I., Crivelli, L., Edwards-Garavoglia, S., Spranger, A., Wittenbecher, F., & Quentin, W. (2015). Switzerland: Health system review. *Health Systems in Transition, 17*(4), 1–288.

Deephouse, D. L., Bundy, J., Tost, L. P., & Suchman, M. C. (2017). Organizational legitimacy: Six key questions. *The SAGE Handbook of Organizational Institutionalism, 4*(2), 27–54.

Diekmann, A. (2002). Empirische Sozialforschung. *Grundlagen, Methoden, Anwendungen*. Reinbek: Rowohlt.

Díez-Martín, F., Blanco-González, A., & Díez-de-Castro, E. (2021). Measuring a scientifically multifaceted concept. The jungle of organizational legitimacy. *European Research on Management and Business Economics, 27*(1), 100131.

Frey, F. J. (2017). Swiss institute for translational and entrepreneurial medicine (sitem-insel). *Clinical and Translational Neuroscience, 1*(1), 2514183X17714101.

Ilgenstein, S. A. (2021). One for the money, two for the show: What are the actor-based incentives for public-private partnerships for innovation? *European Policy Analysis* (early online). https://doi.org/10.1002/epa2.1131.

Langley, A., & Klag, M. (2019). Being where? Navigating the involvement paradox in qualitative research accounts. *Organizational Research Methods, 22*(2), 515–538.

Lengauer, D., & Ruckstuhl, L. (2017). *Compliance*. Schulthess Juristische Medien.

Meynhardt, T., & Jasinenko, A. (2020). Measuring public value: Scale development and construct validation. *International Public Management Journal, 24*(2), 222–249.

Naroll, R. (1965). Galton's problem: The logic of cross-cultural analysis. *Social Research*, 428–451.

Pozen, R., & Kline, H. (2011). Defining success for translational research organizations. *Science Translational Medicine, 3*(94), 94cm20.

Rosser, C., Sager, F., & Leib, S. L. (2020). Six recommendations to build legitimacy for translational research organizations. *Frontiers in Medicine, 7*.

Rosser, C. Ilgenstein, S. A., & Sager F. (2021). The iterative process of legitimacy-building in hybrid organizations. *Administration & Society*, 1–30 (early online). https://doi.org/10.1177/00953997211055102.

Sager, F., & Rosser, C. (2015). Historical methods. In *Routledge handbook of interpretive political science* (pp. 211–222). Routledge.

Seawright, J., & Gerring, J. (2008). Case selection techniques in case study research: A menu of qualitative and quantitative options. *Political Research Quarterly, 61*(2), 294–308.

sitem-insel. (2021, May). *sitem-insel Annual Report 2020*. [Internal document].

sitem-insel. (2022a). *sitem-insel Annual Report 2021*. [Internal document].

sitem-insel. (2022b). *Yearly Report 2021 to the SERI*. [Internal document].

Spano, A. (2014). How do we measure public value? From theory to practice. In *Public value management, measurement and reporting*. Emerald Group Publishing Limited.

Suchman, M. C. (1995). Managing legitimacy: Strategic and institutional approaches. *Academy of Management Review, 20*(3), 571–610.

Swiss Science Council (SSC). (2020). Begutachtung der Mehrjahrespläne nach Art. *15 FIFG für die BFI-Periode 2021–2024*. Schweizerische Eidgenossenschaft.

4

The Journey of the Sitem-Insel and the SCDH

The emergence of the sitem-insel and, a few years later, the SCDH may be traced back to 2008, when the national fiscal equalization scheme between the Swiss cantons was adopted. According to the scheme, the economically strong cantons and the federal government help the financially weaker cantons to strengthen their economic performance (FAA, 2021). While Bern has traditionally been one of the highest receiving cantons, Zurich and Geneva, for instance, have been among the most important donors. For example, the Swiss Federal Institutes of Technology in Zurich and Lausanne generate huge innovative momentum with global appeal and at the same time receive high amounts of federal subsidies. This partly explains why the metropolitan regions of Zurich and of Lake Geneva have clear locational and financial advantages over Bern, especially in the fields of research and innovation (Ilgenstein, 2021).

The new "Swiss Spatial Concept" provided another context for the creation of new research institutions in the canton of Bern. In contrast to the regions of Zurich, Basel, and Geneva, Bern was 2008 not pictured as a metropolitan region in its own right (Ilgenstein, 2021). Rather, the Swiss capital region was considered to occupy "a special position as a center for politics and administration. Thanks to its functions as a political center and bridge between the various parts of the country, it ensures that the state and the economy function properly" (Federal Council, 2012, 75).

Bern was repeatedly put in the public eye as a negative example, which explains why the need for political action grew and became concrete around 2014. In autumn 2014, the canton of Bern's Government Council reported to its parliament that the pharmaceutical and medtech industry had developed dynamically between 2009 and 2014 and that this industry was important for the wealth creation of the canton. However, as the government council added, the industry was underrepresented in the canton of Bern in countrywide comparison. As a result, the government wanted to find ways of how to make the Bernese medtech industry more important in national comparison. To put it in terms of the coordinate system of Fig. 4.1, the aim was to move the medtech "bubble" from the first quadrant to the second quadrant (see shaded arrow and circle).

It is in the context of federal economic competition that the spark for the sitem-insel and the SCDH ignited (Canton of Bern, 2014a, 2014b; Task Force Medicine Bern, 2013). As research institutions of national importance, both organizations are expected to increase the canton of Bern's competitiveness with the help of "medicine" and "healthcare" as unique selling points (USP) (Canton of Bern, 2015, 4; 2021a, 2021b, 2; Rosser et al., 2021).

We now turn to the development of the two hybrids. We start with the sitem-insel, whose story may be summarized as a journey with tailwinds and headwinds.

4.1 The Sitem-Insel: A Journey with Tailwinds and Headwinds

The Swiss Institute for Translational and Entrepreneurial Medicine (sitem-insel) is a research institution of national importance and international appeal (Ammann, 2021).[1]

---

[1] Quote from Christoph Ammann, Minister of Economic Affairs and Member of the Government of the Canton of Bern. See www.sitem-insel.ch (last access: 7.7.2022).

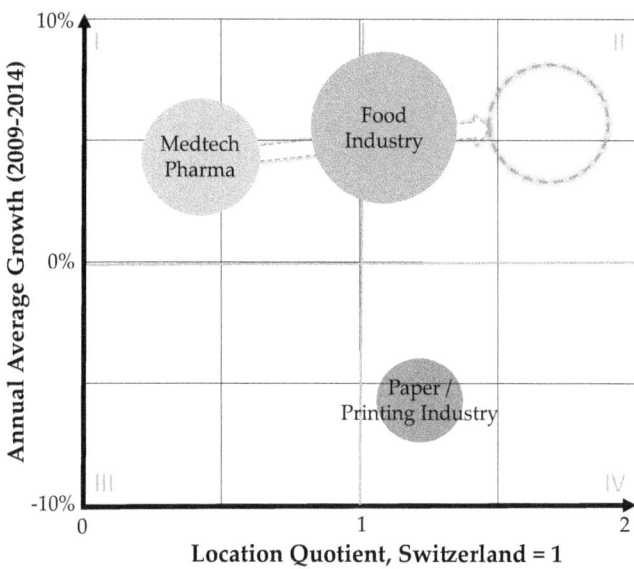

Fig. 4.1 Relevance and Development of the Canton of Bern's Industry by Sector. Source: Adapted from Canton of Bern (2014a, 3). The location quotient on the x-axis measures the importance of the industry in the canton of Bern relative to Switzerland. The y-axis depicts the annual average growth 2009–2014. The food industry as well as the paper and printing industry are depicted as reference for comparison. The circles' diameter illustrates the share of gross value added (GVA) in the total economy, with the medtech and pharma circle representing approximately 1.4%. The shaded arrow and circle symbolize the political aim of the canton of Bern to 'grow' the pharma and medtech circle from the first quadrant to the second quadrant

The period of tailwind corresponds with the sitem-insel's establishment and expansion phase roughly from 2014 to 2019 including several milestones that strengthened the overall development of the hybrid organization. The sitem-insel set sail with the overarching goal to promote translational medicine by connecting people. Translational medicine has at a global scale become important for industry, medicine as well as innovation policy, health policy, and economic policy (Collins, 2011). The translational process describes the transformation of new results from basic research and industrial research and development (R&D) activities into clinical applications (Frey, 2017; Ledford, 2008). Scientific and clinical issues as well as regulatory, educational, entrepreneurial, and economic issues must be addressed simultaneously during this innovation process (Rosser et al., 2020). This is why the translational "two-way road from bench-to-bedside and bedside-to-bench" (Wang et al., 2011, 3) requires a high degree of integration, collaboration, and coordination between industry, science, clinics, regulatory authorities, and other stakeholders (Bornstein & Licinio, 2011, 1567). However, what we observe in reality is a lack of integration, collaboration, and coordination (Mankoff et al., 2004, 2; Rosser et al., 2021). As a consequence, translational research organizations have been founded throughout the world to address this challenge and to increase the impact of medical innovation (Pozen & Kline, 2011; Shahzad et al., 2011).

Representatives from both the public and the private sectors closed the ranks in 2014 to establish the sitem-insel as a nonprofit corporation (Frey, 2017; Rosser et al., 2020). When the sitem-insel was formally established, the shareholders included the Association of Chief Physicians (head of clinics) of the Bernese University Hospital (Inselspital), the University of Bern, the Bern University of Applied Sciences, the Inselspital Foundation, and a global biotechnology corporation with a long tradition in Bern. Following the latter's example, other private sector shareholders followed until the share capital grew from an initial CHF 5.5 million to the current level of CHF 13.6 million (sitem-insel, 2018b, 2021a, 2022a, 2022b).

The formal establishment of the sitem-insel was followed by an intensive phase of preparation for the funding applications to the Swiss Confederation and the canton of Bern. When the application was formally submitted in June 2015, the cantonal jurisdiction lacked a legal basis to draw level with the federal government and subsidize a national institute under the roof of a cantonal innovation promotion act. In fact, the adoption of the respective cantonal law in 2016 was causally linked to the establishment of the sitem-insel (Canton of Bern, 2015, 3). At the end of 2016, the application of the sitem-insel was approved by the federal government and the canton. As stated by Johann Schneider-Ammann, Federal Councilor at that time, the sitem-insel represented a "a future-oriented project [that was] exactly in the focus of the innovation policy of the Swiss Confederation." "Our policy," Schneider-Ammann continued, "calls for collaboration between partners from different industries and research groups and, accordingly, for new models of cooperation. This brings us back to sitem-insel, a model project ensuring the involvement of all partners" (sitem-insel, 2018a, 4).

The operational start of the sitem-insel took place in early 2017 under the leadership of an experienced former head of clinic of the Inselspital and expert in research policy as managing director (sitem-insel, 2018b; Ilgenstein, 2021). The vast construction project of the new facility left its mark on the early development of the hybrid. The building's foundation stone was laid in June 2017. The location at the door to the Insel Campus Bern was and remains to be a decisive asset, since the sitem-insel is within walking distance of nearly all clinical disciplines of the university hospital (Rosser et al., 2020; sitem-insel, 2022a). The highly representative new facility was made ready in May 2019 for the first tenants to move in, a few months before the official opening took place. At about the same time the second application for the funding period 2021–2024 was submitted to the Swiss Confederation and the canton of Bern. After approximately CHF 50 million of subsidies had been granted for the first funding phase (2017–2020), the requested sum now amounted to around CHF 11.2 million. Both the Federal Council and the canton of Bern once more approved the application (sitem-insel, 2019a, 2020a, 2020b).

While the sitem-insel's construction project absorbed a large part of the financial, human, and time resources, additional attention was devoted at the strategic level to engaging new shareholders and including internal and external stakeholders (e.g., new team members, tenants within the building, and members of the broader network). For instance, in view of the high importance of all activities surrounding "Network & Communication" (sitem-insel, 2018b, 15), the Board of Directors decided to recruit a new CEO, who started in November 2018. In general, the sitem-insel's workforce grew from an annual average of approximately 6 full-time equivalents (FTE) in 2017 to approximately 22 FTE at the end of 2021 (sitem-insel, 2022b). While from a total of 26 staff members, nine then worked full time, 17 worked part time, while the number of women amounted to 15, that of their male colleagues was eleven. Three men and three women are presently members of the executive management. This has recently been changed as a result of a restructuring, when two women joined the executive management (sitem-insel, 2021a, 2021b, 2022a).

At the operational level, the sitem-insel had started its threefold core activities. First, the rental of state-of-the-art infrastructure to foster cooperation on a surface of roughly seven small football pitches (appr. 20,000 m^2) was set off successfully with an occupation rate reaching more than 90%. Secondly, the sitem-insel had, together with the University of Bern, begun to provide executive education for future translation specialists with an entrepreneurial spirit. Finally, a professorship for regulatory affairs had with a small team started to conduct research in health economics and regulatory matters (sitem-insel, 2018b, 2019a, 2020a, 2021a, 2022b). The development illustrated thus far was characterized by an iterative approach with a high level of executive room for maneuver; formal structures and processes were specified and implemented parsimoniously (sitem-insel, 2019b, 22).

Similar to the period of tailwind, the period of headwind was heralded by national and cantonal politics. Aside from the obvious impact of the Corona pandemic, two milestones were particularly important in slowing down the development of the sitem-insel (see Fig. 4.2). During and shortly after the official opening of the sitem-insel began the Swiss Science Council's (SSC) audit of the sitem-insel's application for the funding period 2021–2024. The SSC, which advises the federal government on issues regarding research and innovation policy, praised the construction within budget of the sitem-insel's building as an impressive achievement and a lighthouse for the canton of Bern and the Insel Campus (SSC, 2020, 117). On the flip side of the coin was that, according to the SSC (2020), the sitem-insel had so far not achieved its overarching goals of improving the conditions for translational medicine throughout Switzerland and generating additional innovation and value creation at a national scale. The SSC (2020, 117) concluded that the sitem-insel was "not primarily a center for translational and entrepreneurial medicine, but predominantly a real estate company that rents out rooms." Therefore, the SSC recommended that the Confederation should not continue the funding for the period of 2021–2024. Despite the fact that the Federal Council did not follow the recommendation of the SSC and granted the sitem-insel the whole amount of subsidies requested (sitem-insel, 2021a),

4 The Journey of the Sitem-Insel and the SCDH

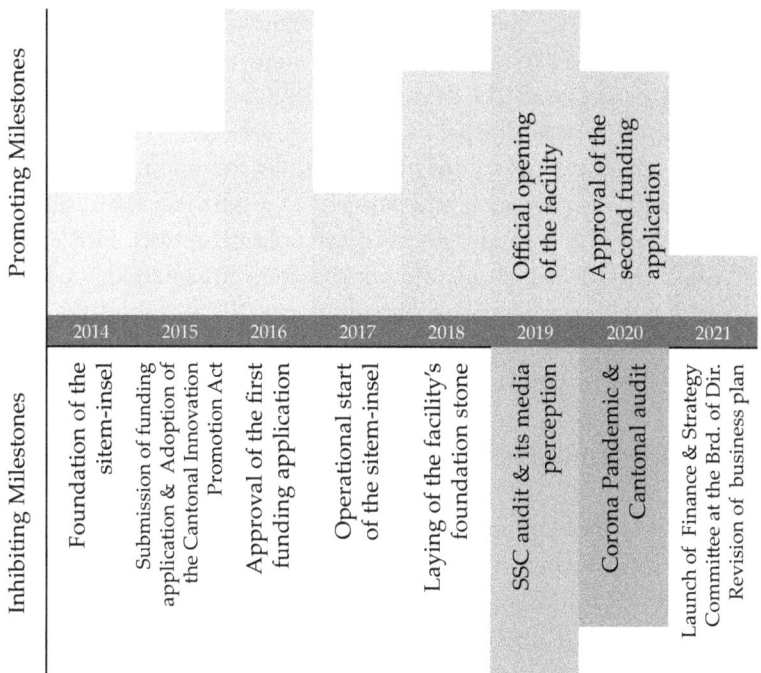

Fig. 4.2 Promoting and inhibiting milestones in the sitem-insel's development. Source: Own illustration. The figure provides a summary of the driving and inhibiting events in the development of the hybrid organization under consideration. The illustration is inspired by Lewin's (1973) "force-field analysis"

a reputational damage occurred. It may not come as a surprise that the local press spoke of a setback for Bern's ambitious flagship project.[2]

The second slowing gust of wind came during 2020 from the cantonal audit office. Belonging to the cantonal public administration, the audit office acts on behalf of both the cantonal legislature and executive and is bound in its activities only by the constitution and the law (Audit Office of the Canton of Bern, 2020; Rosser et al., 2021). In its due process

---

[2] See, for example, www.derbund.ch/rueckschlag-fuer-berns-ehrgeizige-vorzeigeprojekte-980746724275; www.derbund.ch/sitem-insel-will-schwierige-zeiten-hinter-sich-lassen-767063348497; www.bernerzeitung.ch/region/kanton-bern/hoher-investitionsbedarf-berner-regierung-weiter-auf-loesungssuche/story/18793236 (last access: 7.7.2022).

review, the office gave the sitem-insel a worthy report, determining that the canton of Bern's contribution to the sitem-insel was used in accordance with its purpose. The cantonal auditors accredited the sitem-insel to have complied with all legal requirements, all aspects of collaboration, wage and insurance contributions, as well as the applicable principles regarding equal pay for men and women. In a nutshell, the audit report held that there was formally no need for political action. However, the audit office also identified the risk that the sitem-insel would not reach its financial independence and sustainability until 2025 (Audit Office of the Canton of Bern, 10). Obviously, this conclusion was brought to the attention of both the cantonal government and, more importantly, the parliament.

The political and media perception of the sitem-insel changed from high expectations to a certain skepticism around 2020 (Canton of Bern, 2020).[3] When the economic development of the sitem-insel suffered an additional setback due to the Corona pandemic, the Board of Directors of the sitem-insel took measures to strengthen the financial integrity of the organization. In 2020, the Board of Directors decided to form a Finance Committee as well as a Strategic Committee and to make them operational as of 2021 (sitem-insel, 2021a, 2022a). To use a sporting analogy, these measures further strengthened both the defense and the offense of the sitem-insel's team. In addition to the recruitment of financial, legal, and entrepreneurial specialists to the Board of Directors, a position in business development was added to the executive management, while other members of the executive management started to further their education in business administration. Additional structural and procedural measures such as an internal control, a systematic risk management, a comprehensive operations management concepts including safety and security guidelines, and a new accounting software were introduced (sitem-insel, 2020a). The business plan for the period of 2021–2025 was revised and presented (sitem-insel, 2021b), a process that is now being repeated on a yearly basis. Within the business plan, the

---

[3] See also: www.derbund.ch/sitem-insel-will-weiteren-aufbau-nach-corona-vorantreiben-575496533326 and www.bernerzeitung.ch/sitem-insel-braucht-neues-geld-136249964909 (last access: 7.7.2022).

tradeoff between social mission and financial sustainability had now explicitly become an identity-defining topic.

4.2 The SCDH: The Combination of Health and Design as USP

The Swiss Center for Design and Health will be Switzerland's foremost center at the interface between design and healthcare, and will have an international impact (SCDH 2021).[4]

Healthcare and healthcare costs are among the greatest social and economic challenges for the Swiss population (Credit Suisse, 2020; De Pietro et al., 2015). Today, patients choose a hospital for outpatient or inpatient treatment based on market criteria rather than in terms of uniform primary care. New infrastructures, processes, services, and products are needed to sustainably improve both health care and its promotion. Design is considered to play a major role in this increasingly consumer-driven healthcare market. This demand in turn leads to more competition between traditional borders of health care provision (Interview 1; Interview 2; Canton of Bern, 2021a, 2–3).

In contrast to the Continental European understanding, the SCDH defines design in a broad Anglo-American sense that goes beyond the everyday understanding of design as "drafting and shaping." Design-based innovations can range, for example, from digital interfaces that support patient communication to novel medical technology products and the design of entire hospitals (Interview 1). These innovations are intended to make the future healthcare system more efficient and less expensive (Canton of Bern, 2021a). Wherever possible, the innovation process ought to be based on scientific evidence and experience, and should include healthcare professionals, clinicians, scholars from different fields, and political decision makers in addition to patients. Similar to translational medicine, integrating heterogeneous actors is at the same time a key success factor and a major challenge. In terms of collaboration,

---

[4] www.scdh.ch (last access: 7.7.2022).

the so-called living lab forms the core of the SCDH, were research, teaching, and further education as well as applied practice are to be united under one roof (Interview 1). In the living lab, theory and practice are expected to work together on current challenges. They are expected to do so at the interface between design, architecture, processes, and health in order to develop practice-relevant solutions. Moreover, the lab serves as a hub where professionals can profit from a comprehensive offer of research-based and applied education and training (Canton of Bern, 2021a). In a nutshell, the living lab ought to prevent the diverse actors involved from being lost in translation.

As in the case of the sitem-insel, the Economic, Environmental and Energy Directorate of the Canton of Bern was the driving political stakeholder during the establishment and early development of the SCDH. In the course of the political search for new research institutions of national importance, an interdisciplinary research group from the Bern University of Applied Sciences entered the scene, which already had broad project experience and a unique international selling point: the scientific combination of health and design (Interview 1). Since 2007, the Bern University of Applied Sciences disposes of an interdisciplinary team from the fields of design, health, architecture, economics, engineering, and computer science, which collaborates closely with groups from the University of Bern as well as national and international partners from the industry and science. According to the government of the canton of Bern (2021a, 3), this experience and expertise should enable the SCDH to develop "design-based solutions for future-oriented healthcare. The SCDH is about improving spaces, environmental conditions and processes through design. Development and research at the SCDH make these more sustainable, cost-efficient, safe, ecological, transparent and innovative. In future, the SCDH will conduct cutting-edge research in research collaborations with practical partners. This will take place close to the market." It is in this context that the cantonal government affirmed its strategic aim "to become Switzerland's leading medical location with international appeal by means of new R&D centers" (Canton of Bern, 2021a, 2). The government also affirmed that the necessary legal conditions for this endeavor had been created with the implementation of the Innovation Promotion Act in 2016.

In June 2019, the SCDH was established as a nonprofit corporation with a four-member board of directors. Similar to the sitem-insel, the SCDH was presented to the outside world as private–public partnership. Another similarity is that the early development phase of both centers was marked by the search for shareholders and partners willing to invest (Interview 1; Rosser et al., 2021). Among the founding shareholders of the SCDH were the Bern University of Applied Sciences, the University of Bern, and the Inselspital. As regards private investors, the SCDH could convince four companies from the health insurance, communication, education, as well as furniture industries to invest. Bound to performance agreements, the SCDH is expected to be financially independent from subsidies by 2030.

After the acquisition of CHF 4.6 million in share capital, the SCDH applied for subsidies from the federal and cantonal authorities. This process took place under the same formal conditions as for sitem-insel. However, in contrast to the sitem-insel, internationally renowned scientific partners were systematically identified and asked successfully to become members of the SCDH Advisory Board, even before the application for subsidies was submitted. As one of our interviewees stated, the stakeholder inclusion formed an early strategic focus, which turned out to be a great accomplishment providing a boost to the early project. The international reputation of the involved research group and the exclusive and somewhat counterintuitive proposition of combining design and health seem to have served as catalysts. Although the Corona pandemic delayed the actual collaboration on the Advisory Board, meetings are planned to discuss the design and development of the SCDH (Interview 1).

In contrast to the sitem-insel, the most noteworthy force inhibiting the SCDH's development was the Swiss Confederation. Although the Bernese cantonal parliament had approved the SCDH's grant application already in December 2019 and thus signaled its commitment (Canton of Bern, 2019), the federal government decided not before 2021 to support the SCDH with CHF 8 million for 2021–2024.[5] The Federal Government appears to have followed the SSC's respective recommendation. In fact,

---

[5] https://www.derbund.ch/22-millionen-fuer-swiss-center-for-design-and-health-in-bern-729569236169 (last access: 7.7.2022).

instead of advising the Confederation to subsidize the center as requested on the basis of the first application, the SSC (2021) recommended that the SCDH be invited to submit a revision.

According to the SSC (2021, 120), the SCDH's gaps to be filled were fourfold: First, the SSC wanted to see a more evident strategy as to how the SCDH would conduct research and include stakeholders at the national level. Second, the SCDH was asked to specify how to ensure the mutual transfer of knowledge between academia and both the public and the private sectors to the benefit of patients. Third, the composition of the SSC's Board of Directors by 2021 ought to be revised especially in terms of more regional diversity. Finally, the fourth recommendation had to do with the recruitment of research staff. The SSC held that the search for appropriate professors as well as the public or private funding of their chairs must ensure that a critical mass of researchers be involved through open calls. Once the SCDH had handed in the revised application, the SSC came to the positive conclusion that the Confederation should support the SCDH with the above-mentioned sum of CHF 8 million for 2021–2024. This recommendation was not without the caveat that the SCDH's activities be consistent with projections for financial independence after 2029 (SSC, 2021).

In view of the federal politics, the Bernese parliament had to reapprove the SCDH's request for subsidies in September 2021. As a Bernese newspaper reported, "not all members of the Grand Council were comfortable pressing the yes button."[6] The mainly conservative critical voices compared the SCDH with the sitem-insel, which had, as illustrated above, come to be observed with a certain skepticism. Some voices criticized, for example, that "the various projects to strengthen the medical location might get a bit out of hand" (Canton of Bern, 2021b, 3). Another parliamentarian asked, why more and more money "was flowing into these centers" and whether it would not be "appropriate to innovate more in

---

[6] https://www.derbund.ch/22-millionen-fuer-swiss-center-for-design-and-health-in-bern-729569236169 (last access: 7.7.2022).

the rural regions" (Canton of Bern, 2021b, 2). Even though design and health were not seen by several parliamentarians as an obvious marriage in terms of economic benefit, the bill finally passed with a comfortable majority of 103 votes to 23 with 18 abstentions (Canton of Bern, 2021b, 2021c). Curiosity about how design can sustainably improve the healthcare system prevailed. Arguably, the additional federal subsidies of CHF 22 million flowing to Bern until 2029 must have served as additional incentives (Canton of Bern, 2021b). As a consequence, the SCDH was able to declare publicly that both "the Federal Government" and the "Canton of Bern" approve "the funding for the SCDH. "This means that the SCDH will be able to start its operational activities in 2022."[7]

The political delay at the federal level may have had the collateral benefit that the SCDH gained time for the operational development of its organization. For example, an important decision from a financial point of view was not to build a new research building, but to look for a rental property. As the living lab requires a building with high ceilings and generous spaces, the search in Bern turned out to be difficult. As an alternative to the Swiss capital, the SCDH decided to settle in Nidau,[8] a town close to the city of Biel, where a location could be found toward the end of 2021. Here, the University of Applied Sciences, other innovation hubs, and the precision industry have traditionally been present and strong. Finally, the center invested time and energy in expanding its team. At the strategic level, the Board of Directors was further diversified in terms of regional origin, gender, and knowhow. It was also decided to hire professionals with thorough experience in the fields of operational processes and finance. Figure 4.3 summarizes the development of the SCDH illustrated thus far.

---

[7] See www.scdh.ch/en/news-en (last access: 7.7.2022).
[8] See www.scdh.ch/en/news-en (last access: 7.7.2022).

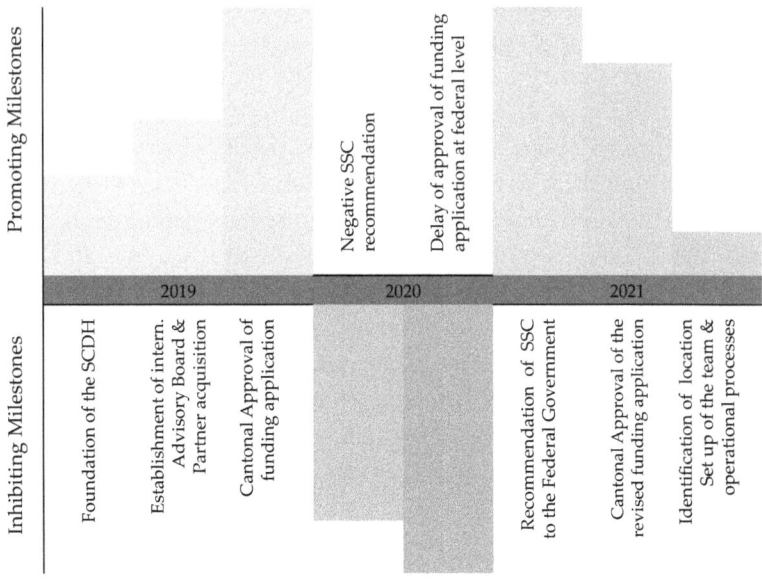

Fig. 4.3 Promoting and inhibiting milestones in the SCDH's development. Source: Own illustration. The figure summarizes the driving and inhibiting events in the development of the hybrid organization under consideration. The figure is inspired by Lewin's (1973) "force-field analysis"

References

Audit Office of the Canton of Bern. (2020). *Activity report 2020*. Audit Office of the Canton of Bern.

Bornstein, S. R., & Licinio, J. (2011). Improving the efficacy of translational medicine by optimally integrating health care, academia and industry. *Nature Medicine, 17*(12), 1567–1569.

Canton of Bern. (2014a, September 2). *Parlamentarischer Vorstoss*. Antwort des Regierungsrates. Geschäftsnummer 2014.RRGR.897.

Canton of Bern. (2014b, October 29). *Richtlinien der Regierungspolitik 2015-2021*. Legislaturziele des Regierungsrates. Geschäftsnummer 2013.RRGR.802.

Canton of Bern. (2015, October 14). *Vortrag der Volkswirtschaftsdirektion*. Dok.-Nr.: 81478.

Canton of Bern. (2019, June 19). *Vortrag der Volkswirtschaftsdirektion*. Swiss Center for Design and Health (SCDH AG); Objektkredit. Dok.-Nr.: 101083.

Canton of Bern. (2020, June 14). *Parlamentarischer Vorstoss. Antwort des Regierungsrats*. Geschäftsnummer 2020.RRGR.252.

Canton of Bern. (2021a, May 12). *Vortrag der Wirtschafts-, Energie- und Umweltdirektion*. Geschäftsnummer 2021.WEU.256.

Canton of Bern. (2021b, September 9). *Wortlautdokument [parliamentary protocol]*. Geschäftsnummer 2021.WEU.256.

Canton of Bern. (2021c, September 9). *Beschlussdokument [parliamentary vote]*. Geschäftsnummer 2021.WEU.256.

Collins, F. S. (2011). Reengineering translational science: The time is right. *Science Translational Medicine, 3*(90), 90cm17-90cm17.

Credit Suisse. (2020). *Sorgenbarometer*. Credit Suisse.

De Pietro, C., Camenzind, P., Sturny, I., Crivelli, L., Edwards-Garavoglia, S., Spranger, A., Wittenbecher, F., & Quentin, W. (2015). Switzerland: Health system review. *Health Systems in Transition, 17*(4), 1–288.

Federal Council. (2012). *Raumkonzept Schweiz*. Schweizerische Eidgenossenschaft.

Federal Finance Administration (FAA). (2021). *Der Nationale Finanzausgleich*. Schweizerische Eidgenossenschaft.

Frey, F. J. (2017). Swiss institute for translational and entrepreneurial medicine (sitem-insel). *Clinical and Translational Neuroscience, 1*(1), 2514183X17714101.

Ilgenstein, S. A. (2021). One for the money, two for the show: What are the actor-based incentives for public-private partnerships for innovation? *European Policy Analysis* (early online). https://doi.org/10.1002/epa2.1131.

Ledford, H. (2008). Translational research: The full cycle. *Nature News, 453*(7197), 843–845.

Mankoff, S. P., Brander, C., Ferrone, S., & Marincola, F. M. (2004). Lost in translation: Obstacles to translational medicine. *Journal of Translational Medicine, 2*(1), 1–5.

Pozen, R., & Kline, H. (2011). Defining success for translational research organizations. *Science Translational Medicine, 3*(94), 94cm20.

Rosser, C., Sager, F., & Leib, S. L. (2020). Six recommendations to build legitimacy for translational research organizations. *Frontiers in Medicine, 7*.

Rosser, C. Ilgenstein, S. A., & Sager F. (2021). The iterative process of legitimacy-building in hybrid organizations. *Administration & Society*, 1–30 (early online). https://doi.org/10.1177/00953997211055102.

Shahzad, A., McLachlan, C. S., Gault, J., Cohrs, R. J., Wang, X., & Köhler, G. (2011). Global translational medicine initiatives and programs. *Translational Biomedicine, 2*(3).
sitem-insel. (2018a). *Information Brochure*. [Internal document].
sitem-insel. (2018b, June). *Yearly Report 2017 to the SERI*. [Internal document].
sitem-insel. (2019a, June). *Yearly Report 2018 to the SERI*. [Internal document].
sitem-insel. (2019b, November 21). Presentation to the Board of Director. [Internal document].
sitem-insel. (2020a, June). *Yearly Report 2019 to the SERI*. [Internal document].
sitem-insel. (2020b, May). *sitem-insel Annual Report 2019*. [Internal document].
sitem-insel. (2021a, May). *sitem-insel Annual Report 2020*. [Internal document].
sitem-insel. (2021b, September). *sitem-insel business plan*. [Internal document].
sitem-insel. (2022a). *sitem-insel Annual Report 2021*. [Internal document].
sitem-insel. (2022b). *Yearly Report 2021 to the SERI*. [Internal document].
Swiss Science Council (SSC). (2020). Begutachtung der Mehrjahrespläne nach Art. *15 FIFG für die BFI-Periode 2021–2024*. Schweizerische Eidgenossenschaft.
Swiss Science Council (SSC). (2021, June 11). *Prise de position du Conseil suisse de la science CSS relative au supplément à la requête du Swiss Center for Design and Health SCDH*. Schweizerische Eidgenossenschaft.
Task Force Medicine Bern. (2013, August 6). *Vision of the "Nationales Kompetenzzentrum für translationale Medizin"* (Translational Medical Center Switzerland – TMCS) [internal document].
Wang, X., Wang, E., & Marincola, F. M. (2011). Translational medicine is developing in China: A new venue for collaboration. *Journal of Translational Medicine, 9*, 3. https://doi.org/10.1186/1479-5876-9-3

5

Legitimacy Building in the Cases of the Sitem-Insel and the SCDH

In the following, we apply our three legitimacy types of governance legitimacy, purpose-rational legitimacy, and value-rational legitimacy as analytical lens to the empirical cases of the sitem-insel and the SCDH. From a descriptive-analytical perspective, we illustrate what has been undertaken by the two hybrids to build legitimacy. From a consultative (or normative) perspective, we also discuss what should have been or will have to be undertaken to increase the two hybrids' level of organizational legitimacy. On the whole, we aim to provide a comprehensive answer to our research questions:

- How do managerial attempts or the lack thereof affect the development of legitimacy in hybrid organizations during their emergence and early development?
- And how should the strategic leadership of a hybrid organization, such as the board of directors or the executive management, systematically and actively manage their organization's legitimacy?

In line with the theoretical section, we first look into how our two cases of hybridity have built governance legitimacy, before we continue with purpose-rational legitimacy and value-rational legitimacy. Our analysis will culminate in our legitimacy guideline at the end of this chapter. By means of the guideline, we hope to offer a practical contribution to the conscious, systematic, and more effective management of legitimacy as a key factor for the success of hybrid organizations.

5.1 Governance Legitimacy: Where Waterfall and Iteration Meet

As stated earlier, governance legitimacy goes hand in hand with the formal aspects of a hybrid organization. This type of legitimacy occurs when a hybrid is run in compliance with the law as well as extra- and intra-organizational regulations, following defined processes, and being led accordingly by the hybrid's management. Governance legitimacy encompasses accountability to defined organizational guidelines and norms, fulfilling formal requirements, establishing necessary facilities and infrastructures, and ensuring sound organizational structures and practices.

5.1.1 Law Abidance and Political Accountability

First, choosing the right legal status is key. According to our interviewees, an important step in their organization's development was the choice of a suitable legal status (Interview 2; Interview 3; Interview 4). This is especially important due to the relative novelty of the hybrids in Switzerland's innovation policy field. According to one of our interviewees, the different possible choices were the legal form of an association, a foundation, or a corporation (Interview 2). For both the sitem-insel and the SCDH, the legal status of a nonprofit limited company under private law was considered most suitable, as it yields the highest degree of economic flexibility (Interview 2). Not only does this legal form allow for a shareholder model and thus future investments from both the public and the private sectors; it also permits the reception of government subsidies and enables optional status changes to a profit-oriented corporation once economic self-sufficiency is achieved (Interview 1; Interview 2). Furthermore, the legal status of a nonprofit limited corporation positively affects the hybrids' perception amongst relevant stakeholders, such as government bodies. Both our cases indicate that the chosen legal status laid the foundation for both hybrids, amongst other factors, to be upgraded to research institutions of national importance (Interview 1). Finally, the status as corporations forced both hybrids to establish a board of directors (Interview 1). Arguably, this inspires confidence in the governance of an emerging hybrid organization.

Second, compliance with legal regulations is of utmost importance (Interview 3; Interview 4). The semipublic nature of hybrids and their reliance on government funding serves as an incentive to know, understand, and follow legal regulations—a fairly self-evident incentive that is even stronger for hybrids than for private companies. Attention must only be drawn to the Swiss postbus scandal, the Berlin Brandenburg airport construction delays, or the exorbitant costs of the Hamburg Philharmonic Opera Hall to get a feeling of how exposed public–private partnerships actually are to the general public. It is thus obvious that malpractice, fraud, misappropriation, corruption, or even delays in the management of key projects are detrimental to legitimacy.

Third, compliance with political requests in general and with political performance agreements, in particular, is essential. Both must be done within the time limits provided (Interview 3; Interview 4). Not only the fulfillment of performance agreements with the Swiss Confederation and the canton of Bern, which are monitored annually by means of comprehensive reports, but also the meeting of accounting standards are necessities that emerging hybrids need to respect. Compiling yearly political reports, performance and compliance statements, as well as financial statements rank among the most important tasks in terms of political accountability (Interview 3; Interview 4). In addition, the timely delivery of the yearly reports to the canton of Bern and the Swiss Confederation are essential (Interview 3; Interview 4). Once submitted, the reports are discussed with the cantonal and, to a lesser degree, federal authorities. In fact, we notice that the Confederation takes a more observing, passive stance, while cantonal representatives steer the yearly evaluation much more actively. Although this might seem obvious, our analysis suggests that due to the importance and yearly recurrence of political reporting procedures, emerging hybrids benefit from an early establishment of robust performance indicators and in-house expertise in accounting and finance. Our interviewees from the SCDH confirm how crucial it is to hire such specialists at an early stage (Interview 3; Interview 4). Professional expertise in accounting and finance are given the highest priority, followed by (mainly ICT-related) operational processes, and risk management topics.

5.1.2 Facility and Infrastructure

Having a representative location and state-of-the-art infrastructure is important (Interview 3). Our interviewees confirm that the attractiveness of their organization is significantly tied to the living lab as infrastructural core of the SCDH (Interview 1; Interview 3). To effectively position themselves as promoters of innovation in the policy fields of research, education, and health, both the sitem-insel and the SCDH rely on state-of-the-art infrastructure. Attractive laboratories, office spaces, training facilities, and meeting rooms allow them to cater to the R&D needs of their stakeholders, for instance, by catalyzing collaboration.

It appears to us that a representative location was particularly important in boosting the sitem-insel's perception as a serious player in the Bernese innovation system. As mentioned above, the sitem-insel's emerging phase was strongly marked by the construction project. Many informal exchanges with internal and external stakeholders reveal that the ability of the sitem-insel's founders to locate the new building project at the entrance to the Insel Campus Bern was a huge success. In other words, it is generally perceived to be critical to the mission of the sitem-insel that the latter operates within walking distance of Switzerland's largest university hospital and medical faculty (Rosser et al., 2020, 2021). However, one of our interview partners states that while the location on the Insel Campus in Bern is vital for the sitem-insel, such an undertaking could also be realized with a somewhat less expensive facility and a top-notch infrastructure (Interview 4).

In contrast to the heavy emphasis of the sitem-insel to build its own property, the SCDH decided to rent a facility. One of our interviewees holds, for instance, that "the SCDH is in a better starting position than the sitem-insel, because it does not have to build its own facility from scratch. Everybody is glad that this is not being done now" (Interview 2). Despite the intention to rent, the search for an appropriate location turned out to be a bigger challenge than anybody would have expected. Due to the lack of satisfying options in the city of Bern, the representatives of the SCDH decided to look out for an alternative solution in the area of Biel—the canton's second largest city (Interview 1; Interview 3). Considering that the Switzerland Innovation Park Biel-Bienne,[1] another hybrid initiative, and the Bern University of Applied Sciences are also located in Biel, the SCDH's leadership expects a campus effect that will not only promote the innovation ecosystem of that area, but that of the entire canton (Interview 2). Above all, the newly found premises satisfy the SCDH's need to build a living lab. This will provide for research projects that may replicate patient rooms or even entire hospital wards (Interview 1), thereby boosting the credibility and reputation of the SCDH.

5.1.3 Leadership and Organizational Structure

In terms of formal leadership and organizational structure, the meaning of the mere presence of leadership bodies such as the Board of Directors, the scientific advisory board, and the executive management can hardly be overestimated (Interview 1; Interview 3). The representation of political-administrative stakeholders in the Board of Directors is one of the peculiarities of hybrid organizations. One of our interviewees holds that even though they need not necessarily be members of the Board of Directors, institutionalized forms of exchange are of high priority for the governance of the organization (Interview 4). What is more, hybrid organizations need a comparatively high degree of diversity in their strategic steering bodies (Interview 3). Not only should they include representatives of the key stakeholders, but also ambassadors with financial and

---

[1] www.switzerland-innovation.com (last access: 7.7.2022).

entrepreneurial credibility and appeal (Interview 3; Interview 4; Rosser et al., 2020, 2021).

As regards the sitem-insel, the vital importance of the political-administrative support in the establishment and further development of the organization has already been illustrated. Another vital early move was the inclusion of the university hospital's head of clinics as major shareholder, quite simply because translational medicine does not work without clinical physicians (Rosser et al., 2020). Later on, the Board of Directors was diversified with both female and male personalities that dispose of an impressive track record in corporate finance and strategic entrepreneurship (sitem-insel, 2021a). Another typical feature of hybrids is their public-private ownership structure. Whereas in the case of the sitem-insel, approximately 30 percent of the investments stem from public shareholders and 70 percent from the private sector, the SCDH's ratio includes 35 and 65% of private and public shares, respectively (sitem-insel, 2022a, 18; Canton of Bern, 2021, 6).

In the case of the SCDH, the importance of including major stakeholders may be exemplified with the following episode (Interview 1). After submitting its application for federal and cantonal subsidies, the SCDH planned an expansion of its board of directors. The initial idea was to increase the level of expertise and experience with a board that was strictly defined by content, which obviously called for the inclusion of more specialists from the domain of design and health. However, the board eventually realized that the main shareholders ought to be incorporated into the Board of Directors (Interview 1). Once the representatives of the SCDH approached these shareholders with specific persona requests, it was no longer difficult to have shareholders elect board members with substantive expertise (Interview 1; Interview 3). Finally, increasing geographic and gender diversity in the board members was another accomplishment. The SCDH was able to do justice to both the requirements of Swiss federalism and gender diversity by acquiring a female member of the federal parliament from the French speaking canton of Vaud as well as a research partner from the Swiss Tropical and Public Health Institute in Basel (Interview 1; Interview 2; Interview 3).

5.1.4 Organizational Processes and Practices

Finally, the question should be addressed as to how important it is to have statutes (articles of association) and formal regulations for organizational governance. As regards the sitem-insel, it is reported that the organization has from both a qualitative and a quantitative perspective reached a good level of formalization (Interview 4). Rather than an isomorphic approach, the sitem-insel followed an iterative approach in compiling formal processes and practices. In addition to the legally binding statutes, for instance, organizational, financial, human resource, and operational management regulations as well as a standardized risk management were gradually compiled and approved by either the Board of Directors or the executive management. As far as ethical standards are concerned, the sitem-insel's official annual report 2021 included information on corporate social responsibility for the first time. Employee satisfaction and retention were now featured explicitly, as were corporate values such as transparency, fairness, trust, team spirit, gender equality, and environmental awareness. Consequently, the annual report stated, "we want to achieve economic growth with sustainable, ethical, and responsible actions" (sitem-insel, 2022a, 16).

In the case of the SCDH, the process of formalizing organizational processes and practices as well as adopting respective regulatory documents is still in its early stages (Interview 1). One interviewee of the SCDH admits a certain ambivalence between the need for formalization, on the one hand, and keeping as much room for maneuver as possible on the other (Interview 3). The current absence of formally approved articles of association represents an example of this tradeoff that was reported during one of our interviews (Interview 3). Having an organizational compliance system in terms of legal, financial, risk, and ICT-related issues as well as human resources and certain ethical guidelines are nonetheless considered to be relevant but maybe not the most urgent issues (Interview 4).

Our research suggests that the formalization of a hybrid's processes and practices is usually triggered step by step by outside impulses. This may—somewhat counterintuitively—lead to more formalism than intended. To make an abstract example, we argue that a request for any given compliance leads to a suspicious reaction whenever a relevant document does not exist. This suspicion in turn incentivizes an organizational overperformance in responding to the initial request. If, however, the requested compliance document is already in place, the request can be satisfied more easily. It is then rather like ticking a box. Finding the right balance between usefully efficient and formalistic regulations is therefore crucial for emerging hybrids (Rosser et al., 2021). We recommend that the level of formalization be a result of an intentional and proactive choice at the leadership level, rather than a mere iterative reaction. The classic waterfall method of project management, consisting of systematically planned and sequential phases, thus maintains its validity when it comes to building governance legitimacy. Even though the security and productivity of a hybrid organization undoubtedly depend on a certain formalization, it is equally important for the leadership of a hybrid to identify the formalities that are superfluous. Otherwise, too much formalization may slow down organizational development.

5.2 Purpose-Rational Legitimacy: Defense Wins Games—Offense Wins Championships

Purpose-rational legitimacy refers to the performance of hybrids and the output they create. As will become clear in the following paragraphs, purpose-rational legitimacy largely refers to the business side of a hybrid organization. A hybrid gains purpose-rational legitimacy when its services serve its stakeholders' instrumental interests. A sporting analogy applies in this context: while games are won on the defense of a hybrid, it is its offense that wins the championship.[2] The defense thereby refers to cost-effective operational processes, whereas the offense consists of well-diversified business models ensuring steady revenue streams.

---

[2] Admittedly, in real team sports the saying is usually the other way around: Offense wins games—defense wins championships.

5.2.1 Strategic Management

First, having a clear vision and mission contributes to building purpose-rational legitimacy (Interview 4). An important output of the strategic management of hybrids is vision and mission statements that are easily understood. The sitem-insel's mission, on the one hand, is based on the promotion of innovation in the medical field by connecting and catalyzing a network of various interest groups that participate in the process of translational medicine such as scientists, clinicians, industry representatives, and regulatory bodies. Network access is thus an important USP. What is more, in close collaboration with the University of Bern the sitem-insel aims to build human capital through executive education in the medical field. Accordingly, the sitem-insel both directly and indirectly supports development processes of innovative products and services as well as their faster market access (Rosser et al., 2021). In other words, the output that the sitem-insel creates relies on promoting innovation through the provision of infrastructure, as well as through the steady knowledge transfer between translational stakeholders (sitem-insel, 2020, 2021b).

In the case of the SCDH, an interviewee reports that it is not necessarily a disadvantage if the vision is not sharpened too early (Interview 3). We observe that the SCDH nonetheless works with clear vision and mission. The vision focuses on the establishment of a center of national importance with international appeal that thematically occupies the interface between health and design (Interview 2). In terms of its mission, the center aims to develop evidence-based design solutions for the healthcare sector, thereby rendering healthcare solutions more effective and efficient. According to one of our interviewees, "design has the ability to improve the life of our society as a whole" (Interview 1). This can affect a broad array of products and services, such as hospital design, industrial medtech aggregates in the form of medical chair design, insulin syringe applications or even the design of a syringe itself (Interview 1; Interview 2). To date, no comparable institution exists in Switzerland. This is also true regarding Europe and other parts of the world. Therefore, an essential part of the SCDH's vision is to fill this gap in Switzerland and address unmet needs beyond national borders. The mission of the SCDH is to become operational through government subsidies, have national and potentially international reach and evolve into a self-sustaining corporation within an eight-year period (Interview 2).

Second, despite its half-public nature, a hybrid organization needs a realistic and well-formulated business plan, which must be oriented toward the goal of economic sustainability (Interview 2). Even though the purpose-rational legitimacy of a hybrid stems from comprehensive and solid business plans, our analysis suggests that the vision and mission statements of both hybrids under consideration entail an emphasis on their social mission or public purpose. Especially in the early strategic development of the two hybrids under consideration, the implementation of economic self-sufficiency via comprehensive business plans seems to have attracted less strategic attention (sitem-insel, 2018, 2019, 2020). Instead, heavy emphasis seems to be put on scientific content and macroeconomic goals that are to be achieved in this scientific context, in order to meet the expectations of political-administrative stakeholders. However, such macroeconomic benefits are arguably hard to operationalize through concrete business models at the organizational level.

Third, a hybrid organization should dispose of valid key performance indicators (KPI) (Yemm, 2013, 37–39). To put it differently, KPIs should "measure" what the hybrid is expected to attain. KPIs are important elements of the sitem-insel and the SCDH's performance agreements with the canton of Bern and, to a lesser degree, the Swiss Confederation (Interview 1; Interview 2; Interview 3). It may thus not come as a surprise that, apart from the most important funding indicators regarding rentability, liquidity, and risk, the political KPIs focus on the fulfillment of the two hybrids' social mission of promoting innovation. In the case of the sitem-insel, for instance, KPIs reflecting business performances were barely existent during the early development phase, as the strategic emphases were on political compliance on the one hand, and the construction of the new building on the other. Additional KPIs with respect to revenue targets were only recently brought into play as a result of internal deliberations between members of the Board of Directors and the executive management (sitem-insel, 2021b).

The SCDH does not (yet) work with formalized KPIs (Interview 1; Interview 3). In terms of performance, securing subsidies was thus far one of the main targets. Achieving this target included securing political support at the federal and cantonal levels, acquiring shareholder capital, finding a real estate solution, and hiring key employees (Interview 1; Interview 3). Similarly to the sitem-insel's early development, the SCDH's implicit performance measurement largely relies on aspects of substantial value creation (Interview 1). As already stated, the generation of financial revenue seems to be of a subordinate character.

Since the public funding of hybrid organizations is relatively new territory, it is hardly surprising that conceptual deficits exist at the level of legislation. For instance, a hybrid organization appears to lose its legal status as a funding institution in the federal research and innovation landscape once the formal funding under Art. 15 RIPA has come to an end. Somewhat paradoxically, a hybrid organization thereby loses its status as a public service provider after a maximum of 8 years. This status, however, has represented the hybrid's very raison d'être in the first place, which has naturally attracted much of the intra-organizational energy and extra-organizational attention (sitem-insel, 2021b). In the case of the SCDH, our analysis also indicates that the slow pace of the federal decision-making process in granting an application counteracts the momentum of hybrids (Interview 1; Interview 3). One of our interviewees holds, for example, that "instead of meaningful certainty of expectations, the political process creates pointless uncertainty, which in turn deters investors. That leads to a complication of a project that is already demanding enough" (Interview 2).

On the whole, our research indicates that hybrid organizations would benefit from coordinated performance evaluation at the level of business operations. Especially if it were possible to include political stakeholders in this evaluation at an early stage, an additional positive impulse for the overall efficiency and effectiveness of hybrids would be given. Accordingly, we recommend applying SMART[3] objectives tailored to the needs of hybrids in their emerging phases, which can eventually be translated into

---

[3] SMART objectives are specific, measurable, assignable, relevant, and time bound.

concrete KPIs at a later stage. In general, our research indicates that hybrids may want to work with KPIs more explicitly than implicitly (Rosser et al., 2021).

5.2.2 Financial Sustainability

Purpose-rational legitimacy also stems from a hybrid's capacity to achieve financial sustainability. What hybrids share with any private venture is the existential need to develop economical operational processes and business models with a clear focus on USPs. We use the plural here because the diversification of potential revenue streams reduces cluster risk (Aversa et al., 2017, 3–7). Simply put, hybrids need to clarify from the very beginning what strategies they employ to earn and to save money.

In terms of saving money, one of our interviewees claims that it is necessary to budget sensibly while at the same time making sure that "one does not save oneself to death" (Interview 4). When it comes to cost-efficiency, our explanations have already pointed toward the significance of acquiring financial management expertise at an early stage (Interview 2; Interview 4; Rosser et al., 2021). On the one hand, the recommendation to insource strategically important knowhow reverberates with the sitem-insel's experience, where a certain initial lack of financial, ICT, and facility management capabilities had to be compensated by later extra-efforts of the sitem-insel's staff as well as the outsourcing of mandates. On the other hand, the SCDH is experiencing similar issues. Key positions regarding finance and ICT architecture need to be filled as soon as possible in order to avoid capacity bottlenecks that will slow down the whole operation (Interview 1). From a purpose-rational point of view, hybrids should thus adopt a balanced personnel strategy, as the presence of experienced entrepreneurs and financial specialists in the leadership is equally important as the presence of scientific experts. An additional optional measure to optimize cost-efficiency may be to voluntarily subject a hybrid organization to a full financial audit. Beyond the limited audit required by the law, this measure would arguably have the collateral benefit of gaining additional stakeholder confidence in the businesslike conduct of hybrids. The cantonal policy actually intends to implement this measure, as the sitem-insel will have to pass a full financial audit as part of the 2021–2024 performance agreement (sitem-insel, 2022b).

Another essential catalyst of purpose-rational legitimacy is a hybrid's transparency in the use of public subsidies (Interview 3; Interview 4). As mentioned above, the sitem-insel and the SCDH share a strong focus on their public purpose because their stakeholders predominantly evaluate them in terms of promoting scientific innovation. Accordingly, the question arises of how to ensure transparency in the use of subsidies at all times. In the case of the sitem-insel, customary Swiss accounting standards (e.g., Meyer, 2017, 19–46) were introduced during the hybrid's emerging process, which not only supported the notion that the hybrid organization was run like a private company. This introduction also contributed to account for the appropriate and transparent use of subsidies received from the Swiss Confederation and the canton of Bern. With regard to the SCDH, our survey confirms both the utmost significance of dealing with subsidies in a transparent manner and the relevance of introducing common accounting standards at a relatively early stage (Interview 3).

In terms of making money, it is key to formulate a financial forecast through a straightforward business plan with an emphasis on diversified business models (Interview 3; Interview 4). In the case of the sitem-insel, the COVID-19 pandemic exemplifies that certain revenue streams, such as the organization of events and executive education, can literally collapse from one day to the other. To put it in the words of the local newspaper *Berner Zeitung*, "The Corona crisis hit the sitem-insel at the worst possible moment: during its establishment. Like a start-up company, the new institution currently has no reserves. The sitem-insel has financial problems because of cancelled events and because of corona-related restrictions in training activities."[4] The need for diversified business models leads us back to the early insourcing of strategically relevant knowhow. Not only is it crucial to have a good defensive lineup of financial experts, but also of an offensive lineup in terms of business development (Interview 3; Interview 4). After a view year of experience, the sitem-insel has taken

---

[4] https://www.bernerzeitung.ch/sitem-insel-braucht-neues-geld-136249964909 (Last access: 7.7.2022).

this into account by appointing experienced entrepreneurs to the board of directors and a business developer with an industry background to the executive board. The case of the sitem-insel also suggests that, although a hybrid's business strategy focusing on revenue streams may be somewhat neglected at an early stage, the balance between the "public" social mission and the "private" financial value creation does gradually even out (sitem-insel, 2021a).

Formulating straightforward USPs does not seem to be easy. Being located on the Insel Campus Bern, the sitem-insel has as USP the closest proximity to the University hospital and its clinics (Rosser et al., 2020, 2021). However, it is currently not evident how access to a network of clinicians commuting at slipper distance between research projects and patient care can be monetized. In contrast, the SCDH is seemingly in a better position, as the combination of health and design as core expertise is almost non-existent at an international level. It has been stated that the SCDH will dispose of a unique living lab at the center of its operations (Interview 1; Interview 2). As promising as this may be, however, we observe that the exact translation of this USP into actual revenue streams is presently still rather vague. This leads us to believe that especially at an early stage, hybrids do not seem to be perfectly aware of their value proposition, let alone of the various nuances of these propositions and their appeal to different stakeholders. Arguably, a certain cliché may have its factual basis here, namely that the academic action-logic does not necessarily lead into stringent and easily understood business models and USP awareness. When it comes to building purpose-rational legitimacy, we arrive at the reverse conclusion that an entrepreneurial action-logic is critical to the success of a hybrid organization. As any private venture, hybrids must be able to deliver more than just an altruistic promise. In other words, stressing the ethical dimensions of a hybrid endeavor is not enough to "sell" the organization and its services. Arguably, this focus instead leads to a distortion in the perception of stakeholders, who overestimate the rigid budget of a hybrid organization in light of public subsidies. It must be realized that hybrids are doomed to fail without sustainable revenue streams beyond public subsidies.

5.2.3 Collaboration and Uptake

Stakeholder inclusion is key to the survival of hybrids (Interview 3; Interview 4; Rosser et al., 2021). Without partners supporting a hybrid, the latter simply cannot perform. This is especially true for platform organizations like the sitem-insel and the SCDH. Stakeholder inclusion can be supported, for instance, by measuring, visualizing, and communicating the extent to which the network generates instrumental value. As regards the SCDH, one interviewee states that "we need a vast network of partners, not just in the sense of donors, but in the sense of partners who support us and contribute to our endeavor with concrete projects" (Interview 1). When it comes to donorship, acquiring stock capital is obviously pivotal for the economic health of a hybrid and, as a consequence, for purpose-rational legitimacy. However, the answers of our interviewees as to how important it is to dispose of a systematic shareholder strategy remain ambivalent (interview 3; Interview 4).

In any case, an extensive network of partners affects hybrids in several positive ways (Interview 3; Interview 4). Most importantly, it creates so-called "legitimacy spillovers" (Kostova et al., 2008, 1001; Rosser et al., 2021) due to social comparison. Someone is quite simply more likely to believe in the instrumental benefit of an organization's services if others believe in and act upon this benefit as well. Having a network including industry partners, for example, anchors a hybrid's endeavor in an economic context, which in turn contributes to convincing politicians of the hybrid's utility. The more partners participate in a hybrid project, the more will the hybrid's value proposition be disseminated to yet other parties (Interview 1). This sets in motion a positive spiral of stakeholder inclusion.

Stakeholder inclusion can be managed. The sitem-insel, on the one hand, has quite deliberately pursued a process-oriented stakeholder inclusion by first bringing local first movers on board before continuing the search for additional partners at the national and international levels (Rosser et al., 2021). In a similar vein, the SCDH envisions to attract local commercial partners from the pharma and medical sectors first and to subsequently attract stakeholders at a national and an international scale. "If you can generate partners locally," one interviewee states, "you can attract other partners. There will be a ripple effect for the location" (Interview 1). On the whole, it is certainly no exaggeration to say that hybrids need to move both stakeholder and shareholder inclusion to the center of their strategies.

5.3 Value-Rational Legitimacy: Visualize Cohesion and Success

Value-rational legitimacy encompasses moral, ethical, and social perceptions of organizations. It is attained when organizations are considered to generate value for the common good. To put it differently, value-rational legitimacy occurs when hybrids are doing the right thing such as giving back to society, thereby exceeding the general expectations of stakeholders.

5.3.1 Social Mission

In order to enjoy value-rational legitimacy, hybrid organizations need to have a social mission or public purpose that is unique and easily understood (Interview 3; Interview 4). In other words, a hybrid organization depends heavily on its social value proposition and the capacity to communicate how effectively it delivers on its social promise.

Although the missions of the two hybrids under consideration have social significance, we observe that both the sitem-insel and the SCDH experience some difficulties when it comes to explaining the concrete social benefit of their centers concisely. For example, it is not easy for the SCDH to express its social mission to a broader audience in an easily accessible way. This may be due to the fact that design is often considered costly, purely esthetic, or far away from what really counts in the healthcare sector. According to one of our interviewees, "It is important that this point is well explained. The SCDH has to show that it is not just doing research in an ivory tower, but that it has an impact on the lives of the whole population" (Interview 1). Arguably, the sitem-insel has a slight advantage here because the social benefit of medical innovation is comparatively easy to convey. However, as the SSC's (2020) verdict about the sitem-insel illustrated above suggests, it does not seem to be straightforward to understand how and to what extent the sitem-insel and its network of more or less loose partners are generating innovation in favor of society at large.

Charismatic ambassadorship contributes to bridging the communicative gap between a complex social mission and its palatable presentation (Interview 3; Interview 4; Rosser et al., 2021). Throughout its young history, the sitem-insel has recruited charismatic personalities with a successful track record, reputation, and appeal from hospitals and industry corporates, chief physicians, as well as members of the national parliament to spread the news about the organization and its goals (Rosser et al., 2021). As mentioned earlier, the SCDH followed a similar path by expanding and diversifying its board of directors to include a broad array of influential personalities. Due to the SCDH's unique position in the comparatively young discipline of design-based healthcare, the hybrid was able to form an international advisory board at an early stage and to attract a number of renowned members functioning as ambassadors of the center (Interview 1).

5.3.2 The Symbolic Appeal of Facilities

It has been argued before that formally disposing of a building promotes governance legitimacy. When it comes to building value-rational legitimacy, it is the symbolic appeal of an attractive location that contributes to convincing stakeholders of a hybrid's ability to succeed (Interview 3; Interview 4). For both the sitem-insel and the SCDH their multifunctional facilities represent central platforms on which research, development, teaching, and business take place.

The sitem-insel, on the one hand, inaugurated its new building in 2019—a building that has repeatedly been referred to by various stakeholders as a lighthouse. The facility encompasses cutting-edge research units, state-of-the-art laboratories, representative offices, meeting and lecture rooms as well as coworking spaces on a surface of approximately 22,000 m². It has already been stated that this lighthouse stands on the

Insel Campus Bern in close vicinity to Bern's university hospital (sitem-insel, 2019, 2020). This architectural presence yielded a symbolic effect that can hardly be overestimated in terms of legitimizing the sitem-insel in its early development.

The SCDH, on the other hand, plans to establish a facility built on evidence-based design criteria. The promise of design-based architecture is to be realized in the SCDH's own home. As repeatedly mentioned, the centerpiece of the building is a living lab, which provides research space for hands-on design solutions (Interview 1; Interview 2). The lab will work as a collaboration hub and use innovative exchange formats to bring together companies, healthcare institutions, and R&D partners. The lab will also host educational facilities for different target groups (Canton of Bern, 2021). Especially at an early stage, the sheer supply of facilities contributes to meeting stakeholder expectations. Only later will the state-of-the-art infrastructure have to prove that it generates a steady and sustainable flow of customers, projects, and revenue. To put it differently, the facility will have to prove whether it fosters purpose-rational legitimacy.

However, having an attractive location is not enough (Interview 4). The architectural trump card can only be played in combination with compelling incentives for stakeholders to work together. Interdisciplinary exchange and collaboration between various actors lie at the heart of both the sitem-insel and the SCDH's agendas (Interview 1; sitem-insel, 2019, 2020). Even though the tenant occupancy rate at the sitem-insel is above 95%, the sitem-insel's management plans to incentivize and simplify stakeholder collaboration with the help of a virtual marketplace platform (Interview 4; sitem-insel, 2021b). By offering its partners a low-threshold opportunity to share technical equipment, personnel, knowhow, and other resources, it may be possible for the sitem-insel to build an even stronger network. Although such open innovation-inspired approaches have the potential to stimulate collaboration (Füller et al., 2012), we expect purpose-rational motives to be the primary drivers of collaboration. Consequently, it remains a challenge for the sitem-insel to earn money by connecting people.

5.3.3 Dissemination and Validation

Communication must be tailored to stakeholders (Interview 3; Interview 4). In terms of conveying success stories, a good audience design represents an appropriate instrument for building value-rational legitimacy. Besides engaging influential ambassadors, hybrids can employ communication specialists at an early stage. In general, they have to be aware of the tradeoff between scientific facts and an easily understandable language. When it comes to conveying a social mission to stakeholders and the broader public, the classic door-to-door canvassing is just as much part of the dissemination portfolio of a hybrid organization as a professional branding strategy, reputation management measures, appealing visualizations, or a high degree of digitalization.

In the case of the sitem-insel, a considerable number of public and private network partners have a high innovation output in both quantitative and qualitative terms. However, the challenge for the sitem-insel as a credible innovation incubator lies in the collection, visualization, and succinct communication of this output. This challenge may only be overcome if the sitem-insel's instrumental role as a platform for the respective innovations as well as their societal relevance become visible. An important strategic accomplishment will thus consist in collecting and visualizing the respective data from the R&D units within the network of the sitem-insel. We believe that the SSC (2020) would not have had too many substantive reasons to portray the sitem-insel negatively if the innovation performance of the hybrid's entire network could have been presented as early as 2019—the year of both the SSC's evaluation and the year of the opening of the sitem-insel. In order to account for the innovation capacity of its network, the sitem-insel is currently working on an "innovation meter" that will allow for a pooled innovation performance measurement. This strategic move is supposed to support the compliance of the sitem-insel with its social mission, thereby satisfying political stakeholders and potentially attracting new public and private partners.

Building and sustaining political support is another vital catalyst for the value-rational legitimacy of hybrid organizations (Interview 3; Interview 4; Rosser et al., 2021). It should have become clear that the steady development of the two hybrids under consideration has relied heavily on the political-administrative support at both the federal and the cantonal levels. As our interviewees confirm (Interview 1; Interview 3; Interview 4), this support must be maintained. The active engagement with governmental representatives and, to a lesser extent, with parliamentarians helps both the sitem-insel and the SCDH to keep a respectful and mutually supportive relationship with politics in general, and anticipate possible political crises, in particular.

It was crucial for the SCDH to create political confidence in the economic and social values of their project. While the SCDH's representatives are aware of the utmost importance of political-administrative support (Interview 1; Interview 3), they also find the greatest threat to the development of their venture within the political sphere (Interview 1; Interview 2; Interview 3). Especially at the federal level, the formal procedures that lead to the granting of subsidies are complicated. It is argued that new requirements have been formulated during the application process, which may compromise the reliability of expectations and threatens the very prospect of success.

As it is tricky for hybrids to navigate the political environment, it is advisable to engage with politicians, to create public awareness for the hybrid's social mission, and to convey its strategy for achieving economic sustainability. In comparison to private corporations of similar size and turnover, investing resources in political marketing and lobbying activities is considerably more important for hybrid organizations. To put it somewhat dramatically, failing hybrids will be held accountable by politics. Hybrid leadership thus entails both having a political strategy and a good sense of diplomacy (Rosser et al., 2021).

Finally, as hybrids depend on a wide range of stakeholders, our interviewees confirm that regular formal and informal exchanges with stakeholders should be sought to follow up with their needs and expectations (Interview 3; Interview 4; Rosser et al., 2021). The collection of stakeholder feedback can lead to adjustments of the hybrid's strategy and business conduct. For instance, the sitem-insel created a community board including senior representatives of the main R&D stakeholders that are working within the sitem-insel's premises. The board serves as an exchange platform that provides a feedback loop before important and potentially expensive strategic measures such as the virtual marketplace, the innovation meter, or joint communication measures are being implemented (sitem-insel, 2021c).

5.3.4 Team

In the same vein as private organizations, hybrids benefit from discussing and defining "corporate" values and working on a corporate culture that not only corresponds with the social mission of the hybrid but also with individual values of the hybrid's staff (Interview 3; Interview 4). Working on a corporate culture will stimulate cohesion and diminish silo building. It is neither a secret nor a surprise that silos do not only exist between organizations, but also within organizations. It should have become clear that hybrids are particularly vulnerable to intra-organizational silo building because they naturally incorporate different "private" and "public" mindsets within their workforce.

It has been stated in Chap. 3 that the executive management of the sitem-insel consists of both "private" management positions and "public" research and teaching positions. It has also been mentioned that a potential trade-off exists between these job profiles in terms of both the intrinsic incentives of those who fill the jobs and the extrinsic expectations that are placed on their performance. While a "private" businesslike mindset primarily pursues revenue-generating and cost-saving goals, the "public" R&D mindset may focus on fulfilling the social mission of a hybrid. As our illustration of the cases of the sitem-insel and the SCDH should have demonstrated, financial and entrepreneurial expertise is equally existential for a hybrid organization as substantive expertise about innovation in medicine or design and health (Rosser et al., 2021). When divergent rationalities, mindsets, and interests act as centrifugal forces within a hybrid organization, its culture must promote cohesion (interview 3; Interview 4). However, this may be easier said than done.

In defining corporate values, both the sitem-insel and the SCDH initiated a rather iterative approach. The sitem-insel, on the one hand, published a first set of corporate values in its official annual report for 2020. This may have been an initial step toward an intra-organizational discussion of what the sitem-insel and its team does and should value. The SCDH, on the other hand, held moderated team workshops at a very early stage, which seems to have launched a continuous exchange that has already yielded first results (Interview 1; Interview 3). We would like to underscore those corporate values and a corporate culture do not distinguish hybrids from private or public organizations. However, our analysis suggests that the more the mindsets of a workforce and, probably more importantly, the leaders of an organization differ, the more difficult value congruence becomes. We may thus conclude with Peter Drucker's succinct statement that "culture eats strategy for breakfast."[5] Emerging hybrids will certainly not suffer from an early and inclusive approach to the definition of values, which in turn may enhance staff motivation and lower turnover rates.

In terms of ethical leadership, our research suggests that public service motivation of employees does not seem to play a significant role. The highly educated staff generally have a strong moral awareness that can be utilized to the benefit of the organization. In the two cases observed, an intra-organizational motivational focus seems to be more important for employees than an extra-organizational orientation. More specifically, a start-up mentality—everyone going the extra mile for each other and doing a little bit of everything—seems to be more prevalent and effective than employee motivation focusing on the common good (Heres & Lasthuizen, 2012).

Obviously, sound ethical decisions that take into account different interests and short-term and medium-term consequences are central to the leadership of hybrid organizations. In this context, radical transparency seems to be a more effective strategy that clandestine approaches, which arguably takes courage from a leadership perspective. Leaders of hybrids cannot hide behind formalism; even if it may read stereotypical, they have to "lead by example" and "walk the talk." It should have become clear that both the sitem-insel and the SCDH are small organizations with large public appeal, which is why their leaders can and must be accessible, supportive, trusting, and loyal to their employees.

---

[5] www.forbes.com/sites/forbescoachescouncil/2018/11/20/why-does-culture-eat-strategy-for-breakfast/?sh=227bd5511e09 (last access7.7.2022).

Formally "enforcing" ethical behavior is of no use compared to exemplifying it. Accordingly, management by "walking around" seems a promising leadership approach for hybrid organizations.

With our qualitative analysis, we have prepared the ground for our legitimacy guideline—the actual core of this contribution—which we will now turn to.

5.4 The Legitimacy Guideline

Based on our qualitative empirical analysis illustrated above, we developed a simple guideline with 36 recommendations (see Fig. 5.1). This guideline consists of 16 recommendations for building governance legitimacy, and 11 and 9 recommendations for building purpose-rational legitimacy and value-rational legitimacy, respectively. First, the guideline can be used to assess on a scale of 1–10 how important each recommendation is in relation to a specific hybrid organization. While 1 means completely unimportant, 10 signifies that the recommendation is of the highest relevance for the success of a hybrid. In real situations, individual members of a board of directors or management may either score the importance of the individual items independently or the guideline may be used in strategy meetings or workshops. In strategy meetings, the guideline may also prove helpful to structure the deliberation about the relevance and urgency of concrete measures.

In addition to the relevance of the individual items, it is possible to evaluate the performance of one's own hybrid organization. If the individual relevance scores are then correlated with the individual performance scores, it is quite straightforward to derive the urgency with which measures are to be taken to implement the respective recommendation. The evaluation categories "relevance," "performance," and "urgency" are presented in Appendix C in the form of a tabular checklist. In analogy to the assessment of the relevance of the individual recommendations, the deduction of concrete measures to increase the organizational legitimacy of a hybrid can also happen in the context of strategy meetings—whether

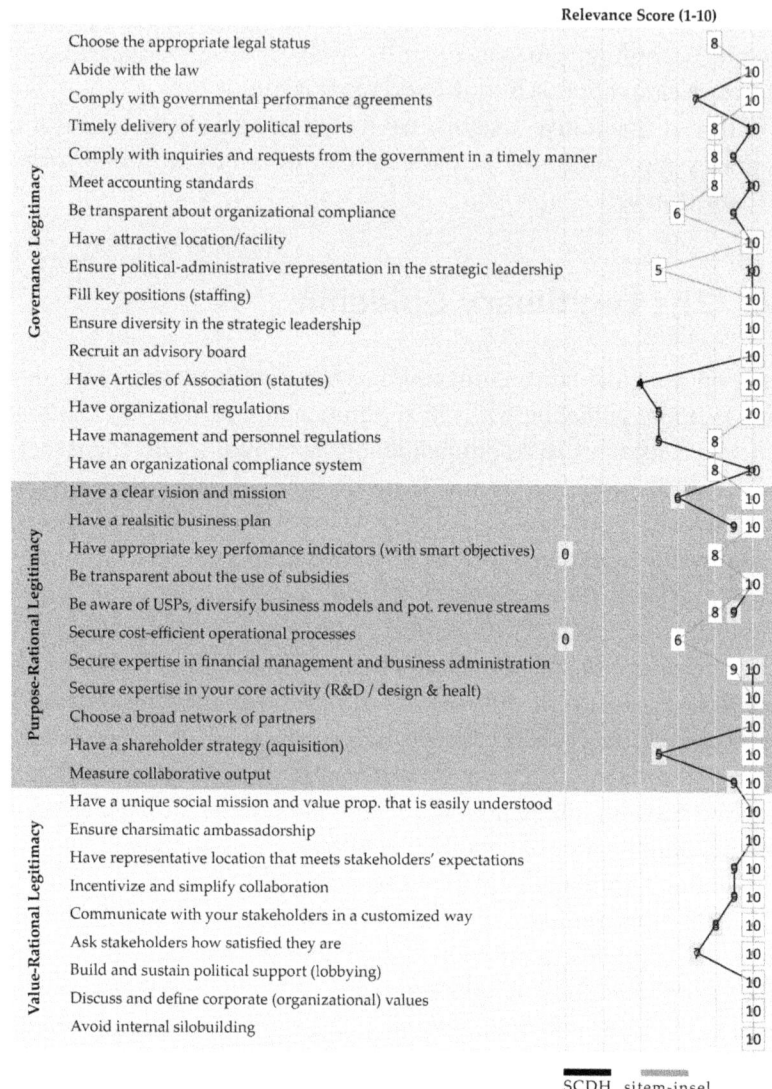

Fig. 5.1 Legitimacy Guideline. Source: Own illustration with the kind support of Angela Tschumi and Ramona Schindler. The two SCDH-related zero values are missing scores. It has been reported that a meaningful estimation of the relevance of the respective items is not yet possible

in the board of directors or the executive management, and whether with or without external moderation.

As described in the methodological section, we asked one representative of the SCDH and one representative of the sitem-insel to estimate the relevance of the individual items for their organization. Figure 5.1 provides an overview of the individual relevance scores. It shows that a large majority of the scores are between 8 and 10, while only ten scores rate lower. The rounded average of the individual scores in the category of governance legitimacy for the SCDH and the sitem-insel are 8.6 and 8.7, respectively, whereas the corresponding averages are 8.7 and 9.2 for purpose-rational legitimacy, and 9.2 and 10 for the category of value-rational legitimacy.

We refrain from interpreting the marginal differences between the average relevance scores of the two organizations, as it seems likely that the differences are a result of individual response behavior. In this context, a survey with a (significantly) higher N would of course be interesting. In the sense of a preliminary test, the high scores illustrated here suggest that the recommendations of the legitimacy guideline are indeed essential drivers of the prospects of a hybrid's success. We refrain here from displaying performance and urgency scores for the SCDH and the sitem-insel. When we discussed the items of our guideline with our two interviewees, we also talked about the performance of the SCDH and the sitem-insel. Instead of displaying corresponding scores, however, we incorporated the valuable feedback gathered during our last two interviews into the empirical analysis illustrated above.

In conclusion, we believe that our legitimacy guideline provides the strategic leadership of a hybrid organization, such as the board of directors or the executive management, with a valid and hands-on tool to manage their organization's legitimacy systematically and actively.

References

Aversa, P., Haefliger, S., & Reza, D. G. (2017). Building a winning business model portfolio. *MIT Sloan Management Review, 58*(4), 49–54.

Canton of Bern. (2021, May 12). *Vortrag der Wirtschafts-,* Energie- und Umweltdirektion. Geschäftsnummer 2021.WEU.256.

Füller, J., Matzler, K., Hutter, K., & Hautz, J. (2012). Consumers' creative talent: Which characteristics qualify consumers for open innovation projects? An exploration of asymmetrical effects. *Creativity and Innovation Management, 21*(3), 247–262.

Heres, L., & Lasthuizen, K. (2012). What's the difference? Ethical leadership in public, hybrid and private sector organizations. *Journal of Change Management, 12*(4), 441–466.

Kostova, T., Roth, K., & Dacin, M. T. (2008). Institutional theory in the study of multinational corporations: A critique and new directions. *Academy of Management Review, 33*(4), 994–1006.

Meyer, C. (2017). *Accounting. Ein Leitfaden für das Verständnis von Finanzberichten.* 2., vollständig überarbeitete Auflage. EXPERT Suisse.

Rosser, C., Sager, F., & Leib, S. L. (2020). Six recommendations to build legitimacy for translational research organizations. *Frontiers in Medicine, 7.*

Rosser, C. Ilgenstein, S. A., & Sager F. (2021). The iterative process of legitimacy-building in hybrid organizations. *Administration & Society,* 1–30 (early online). https://doi.org/10.1177/00953997211055102.

sitem-insel. (2018, June). *Yearly Report 2017 to the SERI.* [Internal document].
sitem-insel. (2019, June). *Yearly Report 2018 to the SERI.* [Internal document].
sitem-insel. (2020, June). *Yearly Report 2019 to the SERI.* [Internal document].
sitem-insel. (2021a, May). *sitem-insel Annual Report 2020.* [Internal document].
sitem-insel. (2021b, September). *sitem-insel business plan.* [Internal document].
sitem-insel. (2021c, October 14). *sitem-insel community board presentation to the kickoff meeting.* [Internal document].
sitem-insel. (2022a). *sitem-insel Annual Report 2021.* [Internal document].
sitem-insel. (2022b). *Yearly Report 2021 to the SERI.* [Internal document].

Swiss Science Council (SSC). (2020). *Begutachtung der Mehrjahrespläne nach Art. 15 FIFG für die BFI-Periode 2021–2024.* Schweizerische Eidgenossenschaft.

Yemm, G. (2013). *Essential guide to leading your team: How to set goals, measure performance and reward talent.* Pearson Education.

6

Conclusion

This contribution has been dedicated to analyzing how emerging hybrid organizations gain legitimacy. Our scholarly starting point was the premise that legitimacy is a vital necessity for the success of organizations and that the aggregated legitimacy of an organization positively correlates with its overall performance (Díez-Martín et al., 2013; Dowling & Pfeffer, 1975; Zimmerman & Zeitz, 2002). We have argued that legitimacy is of even greater importance for hybrids than for private or public organizations, as they must respond to a larger and more heterogeneous stakeholder structure than their non-hybrid sisters (Rosser et al., 2021). Based on these propositions we have addressed both a descriptive-analytical and a consultative (or normative) research question. From a descriptive-analytical perspective, we have illustrated what events and managerial decisions have affected the development of legitimacy in two emerging hybrids. From a consultative (or normative) perspective, we have illustrated what the strategic leadership of hybrids should do to systematically increase the legitimacy of their organization.

In order to operationalize the question of how hybrids may build legitimacy, we have defined a fairly simple and thus applicable legitimacy typology consisting of the three types of governance legitimacy, purpose-rational legitimacy, and value-rational legitimacy. Subsequently, we have applied the typology to two typical cases of hybridity, namely the sitem-insel and the SCDH. The qualitative-comparative comparison of the two cases has culminated in the actual core of this book, namely a hands-on manager's guide to the sweet spot of legitimacy. On the whole, our qualitative-comparative analysis gives way to the conclusion that legitimacy is a logical corollary emanating from the specific management of an array of organizational tasks. In this process, the systematic combination and active implementation of the three mutually reinforcing legitimacy types optimize the overall level of legitimacy in emerging hybrids.

Our research indicates that the conscious, active, and systematic management of legitimacy is a significant aspect to be considered during the establishment process of hybrid organizations. While one can obviously not derive broad generalizations from a comparison of two cases, our research nevertheless suggests that the multifaceted phenomenon of organizational legitimacy may be taken as an overarching structure to unify the relevant success factors of hybrid endeavors. Besides stressing the general importance of organizational legitimacy for the success of hybrids, the analysis of our two cases suggests that building legitimacy is not (yet) a goal per se, but rather something that is achieved indirectly and implicitly.

Turning from such larger strokes to the more specific implications of our work, we believe that several key findings are of both practical and theoretical relevance. From a practical point of view, the descriptive-analytical comparison of the development of the sitem-insel and the SCDH has revealed, for instance, that the opportunity costs of an inception phase dominated by a vast construction project are high. Emerging hybrids are thus well advised to consider infrastructure requirements carefully while at the same time counterbalancing the impact these requirements may have on both a hybrid's fulfillment of the social mission and its quest for financial sustainability. In this context, our comparative analysis suggests that hybrids may learn from each other. For example, it has been shown that the SCDH's decision in favor of rental facilities was influenced by the sitem-insel's pioneering experience with an extensive construction project.

Another important observation is that the need for public accountability comes with subsidies from political authorities. In this context,

6 Conclusion

hybrids seem to operate with a slim margin of error while facing the herculean task of achieving economic self-sufficiency. Unlike private companies of comparable size, hybrid organizations are very much in the public spotlight. As our analysis indicates, public sentiments surrounding hybrids can change rather quickly. This is why managing public expectations, as expressed via political or media discourse, is a central aspect of managing hybrid organizations (Rosser et al., 2021).

Analyzing hybrid organizations through the lens of governance legitimacy reveals how critical formal, legal, and structural aspects are already at an early stage. These aspects include, for instance, choosing the right legal status as well as complying with legal regulations and political performance agreements. Our research also suggests that emerging hybrids benefit from an early establishment of robust performance measures and in-house expertise in accounting and finance as well as operational processes. However, while several formal structures and processes are substantially important and conducive for the successful growth of a hybrid organization, other formalities are more symbolic. Compared to private organizations, hybrids arguably have to fulfill more formal requirements in the sense of "ticking a box." A certain degree of organizational decoupling may then happen without endangering the legitimacy of the organization. In order to preserve intra-organizational flexibility, for instance, it may sometimes be justified to separate formal structure from the actual organizational practice (Meyer & Rowan, 1977). What we would like to stress as take-home message here is that formal organizational structures and processes should be a result of an intentional and proactive choice, rather than mere iterative reaction. We, therefore, conclude that the traditional and somewhat out-of-fashion waterfall method of project management, consisting of systematically planned and sequential phases, maintains its validity when it comes to building governance legitimacy.

In order to build purpose-rational legitimacy, the effectiveness of a hybrid organization's provision of goods and services must be high. Our contribution suggests, for example, how important an accessible mission statement and a realistic business plan including diversified business models are for a hybrid's performance. Our analysis indicates that emerging hybrids tend to emphasize the creation of scientific innovation more imminently, while treating the generation of sustained financial revenue via comprehensive business plans more distantly. However, a key driver for purpose-rational legitimacy is a hybrid's capacity to achieve financial sustainability. As our research suggests, hybrid organizations need to clarify from the very beginning what financial and personnel strategies they employ to earn and save money. Stakeholder inclusion is key in this regard because nothing validates the output of a hybrid more effectively than a large network of partners who have a utility-maximizing interest in the hybrid's products and services.

Finally, hybrid organizations build value-rational legitimacy when they generate notional or intangible value for the common good and effectively deliver on their social promise. Our research suggests that even when following obvious social missions, hybrids may struggle to explain the actual social benefits they create. In order to deal with this challenge of ambiguity, hybrids may want to recruit charismatic personalities as ambassadors. Thanks to the symbolic capital and broad outreach of such ambassadors, the social role of a hybrid organization may be advocated and corresponding goals may be communicated convincingly (Levy et al., 2009, 358). Further actions in terms of building value-rational legitimacy are interdisciplinary collaborations between various actors to create legitimacy spillovers (Kostova et al., 2008). Our results also imply that hybrids may want to employ communication specialists at an early stage to convey their social impact in a professional and effective way to stakeholders and the broader public. In this context, the importance of navigating the political environment to create public awareness for a hybrid's social mission should once more be stressed.

From a theoretical perspective, we contribute to the nascent state of research about legitimacy building in emerging hybrids. For instance, our contribution may complement conventional theoretical frameworks by increasing the operationalizability of legitimacy typologies, thereby increasing their practical usability for managers of hybrids. The illustrated journeys of Bern's hybrid endeavors may effectively serve as blueprints for hybrid ventures to come. Further thorough reflection on how to "measure" organizational performance with abstract and somewhat intangible phenomena such as legitimacy may also enrich other theoretical approaches at the intersection of Business Administration and Public Administration. For example, the public value approach (Meynhardt &

Jasinenko, 2020; Rosser, 2017) or that of administrative reputation (Bustos, 2021; Carpenter & Krause, 2012) are somewhat hybrid fields of study dealing with similar questions. Our research may be considered as humble contribution to start building bridges between these approaches.

Speaking of a humble contribution, we would finally like to address some limitations of our contribution—obviously without being conclusive in any way. Since we have already dealt with the issue of author involvement in a case study, it may suffice to merely mention this limitation again. We would also like to repeat that it is not possible to draw general conclusions from a qualitative case study with two cases. Another limitation stems from the fact that our study has been conducted from an intra-organizational perspective. However, since external actors obviously bestow legitimacy upon organizations, we believe that our findings should be verified through external stakeholder interviews and surveys. Another limitation concerns the case selection. The similarity of both cases in terms of geographical location as well as cultural, political, and legal environments were ideal for the analytical comparison of the two cases and for understanding their within-case complexity. However, comparisons with a broader and more diversified array of examples could potentially shed light on further differences as well as additional best practices for emerging hybrids. In other words, most-similar case scenarios may be complemented with most-different comparisons of hybrids in order to shed more light on the ideal path to the sweet spot of legitimacy.

References

Bustos, E. O. (2021). Organizational reputation in the public administration: A systematic literature review. *Public Administration Review*.

Carpenter, D. P., & Krause, G. A. (2012). Reputation and public administration. *Public Administration Review, 72*(1), 26–32.

Díez-Martín, F., Prado-Roman, C., & Blanco-González, A. (2013). Beyond legitimacy: Legitimacy types and organizational success. *Management Decision., 51*(10), 1954–1969.

Dowling, J., & Pfeffer, J. (1975). Organizational legitimacy: Social values and organizational behavior. *Pacific Sociological Review, 18*(1), 122–136.

Kostova, T., Roth, K., & Dacin, M. T. (2008). Institutional theory in the study of multinational corporations: A critique and new directions. *Academy of Management Review, 33*(4), 994–1006.

Levy, M., Sacks, A., & Tyler, T. (2009). Conceptualizing legitimacy, measuring legitimating beliefs. *American Behavioral Scientist, 53*(3), 354–375.

Meyer, J. W., & Rowan, B. (1977). Institutionalized organizations: Formal structure as myth and ceremony. *American Journal of Sociology, 83*(2), 340–363.

Meynhardt, T., & Jasinenko, A. (2020). Measuring public value: Scale development and construct validation. *International Public Management Journal, 24*(2), 222–249.

Rosser, C. (2017). NPM und Public Value im Spannungsfeld mechanischer und organischer Staatsverständnisse. *Jahrbuch der Schweizerischen Verwaltungswissenschaften, 8*(1), 116–132.

Rosser, C. Ilgenstein, S. A., & Sager F. (2021). The iterative process of legitimacy-building in hybrid organizations. *Administration & Society*, 1–30 (early online). https://doi.org/10.1177/00953997211055102.

Zimmerman, M. A., & Zeitz, G. J. (2002). Beyond survival: Achieving new venture growth by building legitimacy. *Academy of Management Review, 27*(3), 414–431.

Appendix A Empirical Strategy

	Definition	Operationalization	Utterances (non-exhaustive)
Governance legitimacy	Governance legitimacy refers to regulative, technical, and managerial aspects of a hybrid. It occurs when stakeholders perceive organizational procedures, structures, practices, routines, and leadership to be sound and professional	Information about the formal organization (properties)	• Legal structure • Relevant laws and regulations • Performance agreements • Share- and stakeholder structure • Accounting standards • Financial structure and solvency • Facility, infrastructure • Organizational compliance system (internal regulations and directives in fields such as legal, financial, tax-, HR-, safety and security, risk, quality insurance, and IT-related issues • Status and seniority of management, qualification and training of staff, industry experience • Presence of advisory board (and its representativeness)
Purpose-rational legitimacy	Support for a hybrid in anticipation of its instrumental value and the utility of its output	Information about the organization's performance expectation (quantity and quality of products and services)	• Vision and mission • Business plan, strategy of how to earn and safe money (e.g. business models) • Clear objectives, SMART goals, presence of KPIs • Information about the use of public subsidies • HR-strategy • Shareholder strategy • Partnerships, collaborations • Collaborative output (R&D projects, industry funding, etc.)

Value-rational legitimacy	Support for a hybrid's congruence with the normative convictions as well as moral, ethical, and social values held by stakeholders	Information about organizational behavior that is seen as fair, proper, appropriate, or desirable	• Social mission/public purpose • Communicative appearance to the outside world • Support uttered by political-administrative actors • Attractiveness and representativeness of facility and location • Collaborations • Organizational (corporate) values • Team building
Data	\multicolumn{3}{l|}{**Written primary sources (non-exhaustive)**: Statutes, performance agreements, regulations, guidelines, contracts, meeting and workshop protocols, annual reports, funding structure, balance sheet(s), organizational charts, ownership structure (e.g., commercial register entry and share register), business plan, operating license, certifications (e.g., ISO), parliamentary protocols, newspaper articles, etc. **Online information**: Websites, audio and video documents, social media (LinkedIn). **Expert interviews** (see Appendix B)}		

Appendix B Interview Questionnaire

Introductory Questions (Setting the Scene and Getting in the Right Mood)

- Please describe the vision that stands behind the Swiss Center for Design and Health (SCDH) as well as its implementation strategy.
- What are the most challenging obstacles in the implementation of the strategy?
- Please describe the establishment process of the SCDH: What were the main drivers that led to its founding and to the establishment of its leadership? What were the key developments that pushed this process forward?
- Please contextualize and specify the political support the SCDH receives. What is the concrete benefit of this support?

Output-Oriented Questions

- What is the concrete output that the SCDH is creating or aiming to create?
- Who are the main stakeholders and how do or will these groups benefit from the services provided?
- What are your important milestones and key successes thus far?
- How is the SCDH financed and is it sustainable? If not, do you foresee it being financially sustainable in the future?
- Which parameters (KPI) "measure" the success of the Center?

Value-Oriented Questions

- What activities do you do in terms of branding, marketing, and communication?
- What are the main reasons for your stakeholders to support the SCDH and participate in its endeavor?
- Can you describe stakeholder's feedback about the expected services provided by the SCDH? Can you share concrete examples?
- To what extend do these expected services create social impact?
- What values play a central role in the management of the SCDH? To which extend are these values met in daily practice?
- What benefits (if any) does the SCDH provide to its workforce that go beyond salaries?
- What role does environmental, social, and corporate governance (ESG) or corporate social responsibility (CSR) play in the management of the Center?

Governance-Oriented Questions

- Please describe the reporting and regulatory oversight mechanisms of the Center.
- What are the most important skills your staff needs and how do you select staff?

October 2021, C. Pfaff & C. Rosser

Appendix C Legitimacy Guideline

Legitimacy-related recommendation (Item)	Relevance	Performance	Urgency
Choose the appropriate legal status			
Abide with the law			
Comply with governmental performance agreements			
Timely delivery of yearly political reports			
Comply with inquiries and requests from the government in a timely manner			
Meet accounting standards			
Be transparent about organizational compliance			
Have attractive location/facility			
Ensure political-administrative representation in the strategic leadership			
Fill key positions (staffing)			
Ensure diversity in the strategic leadership			
Recruit an advisory board			
Have articles of association (statutes)			
Have organizational regulations			
Have management and personnel regulations			
Have an organizational compliance system			

(continued)

(continued)

Legitimacy-related recommendation (Item)	Relevance	Performance	Urgency
Have a clear vision and mission			
Have a realistic business plan			
Have appropriate key performance indicators (with smart objectives)			
Be transparent about the use of subsidies			
Be aware of USPs, diversify business models and pot. revenue streams			
Secure cost-efficient operational processes			
Secure expertise in financial management and business administration			
Secure expertise in your core activity (R&D/design and health)			
Choose a broad network of partners			
Have a shareholder strategy (acquisition)			
Measure collaborative output			
Have a unique social mission and value prop. that is easily understood			
Ensure charismatic ambassadorship			
Have representative location that meets stakeholders' expectations			
Incentivize and simplify collaboration			
Communicate with your stakeholders in a customized way			
Ask stakeholders how satisfied they are			
Build and sustain political support (lobbying)			
Discuss and define corporate (organizational) values			
Avoid internal silo building			

Whereas the individual legitimacy-related recommendations (items) can be rated from 1 to 10 regarding their relevance for a specific hybrid organization, the performance column can be used to qualitatively evaluate one's own organization in the respective areas with values from 1 to 10. Finally, the urgency with which measures to improve the performance of one's own organization ought to be implemented can also be rated from 1 to 10. 10 is the highest or best value in each column.

Ingram Content Group UK Ltd.
Milton Keynes UK
UKHW040723190623
423418UK00030B/6